A KEY TO THE

CASE-BEARING CADDIS LARVAE OF BRITAIN AND IRELAND

by

I. D. WALLACE★

B. WALLACE★

and

G. N. PHILIPSON†

FRESHWATER BIOLOGICAL ASSOCIATION

SCIENTIFIC PUBLICATION No. 51

1990

Series Editor: J. M. ELLIOT

★ Department of Zoology, Liverpool Museum, William Brown Street, Liverpool, L3 8EN (address for all correspondence).
† Department of Zoology, The University, Newcastle upon Tyne, NE1 7RU.

This publication is sponsored by National Power. A generous contribution has covered most of the production costs and the Freshwater Biological Association is most grateful for the support.

Published by the Freshwater Biological Association,
The Ferry House, Far Sawrey, Ambleside, Cumbria LA22 0LP

in association with

National Museums and Galleries on Merseyside

ISBN 0900386 49 5

ISSN 0367–1887

PREFACE

Caddis larvae that build and carry cases of mineral and plant materials are some of the most conspicuous members of the British freshwater fauna. Nevertheless the ecology of these case-bearers is poorly known because, until recently, it has been difficult or impossible to identify many of the species and the lack of detailed keys for identification has hampered or prevented research on their biology and ecology. This situation will now be redressed, I hope, by the publication of the first FBA key to the case-bearing caddis larvae of Britain and Ireland.

Taxonomic studies on caddis larvae have been greatly advanced by the work of Dr G. N. Philipson and his students at the University of Newcastle upon Tyne, and we are particularly fortunate to have Dr Philipson as co-author of this key with Drs I. D. and B. Wallace, who have an extensive knowledge of the largest and taxonomically difficult family, the Limnephilidae. As a result of their persistent dedication it is now possible to identify most species of case-bearing caddis larvae, and publication of their key should help to stimulate more research on the ecology of these fascinating animals. The key will, I am sure, prove to be a worthy companion for the FBA key to caseless caddis larvae (No. 43 by J. M. Edington & A. G. Hildrew, 1981). Unlike it and other recent FBA Scientific Publications the new key does not have a separate section of ecological notes, although brief mention is made of distributions and habitats at appropriate places in the text. With this minor *caveat emptor* in mind I am certain that all will welcome the long-awaited publication of this key.

The Ferry House   J. G. Jones
November 1989   *Director*

CONTENTS

INTRODUCTION

A 'caddis' is popularly considered to be an aquatic insect living in a portable tube or case which it has made from various materials. There are, however, many caddis-flies whose larvae do not make cases and this difference in habit has resulted in a convenient division of Trichoptera larvae into 'case-bearing' and 'caseless'. Unfortunately, the division is not as precise as one might have hoped. Some 'case-bearing' larvae are caseless until they reach the final instar (Hydroptilidae); others may abandon their cases under certain circumstances and drift without cases in the stream flow (Glossosomatidae); a few, at least in captivity, readily leave and re-enter their cases (Phryganeidae). Conversely, 'caseless' larvae construct fixed shelters of various materials in which they live or pupate; such shelters, dislodged when sampling, may well be found to contain a larva which the unwary might consider to be 'case-bearing'. For such reasons, the families grouped as 'cased' or 'caseless' must be carefully defined on grounds of larval morphology.

It should also be borne in mind that the division of caddis into two groups depending on the presence or absence of a case during the development of the larva is not fully supported by their phylogeny. The division separates the Glossosomatidae and Hydroptilidae from the closely related caseless Rhyacophilidae, three families which are grouped together in the same superfamily.

CHECK-LIST OF CASE-BEARING CADDIS IN BRITAIN AND IRELAND

This check-list is taken from Barnard (1985). Redundant names used by Kimmins (1966) and Macan (1973) are shown in parentheses. Asterisks against species names indicate there are no authenticated records from Ireland (O'Connor 1987; O'Connor & O'Hanrahan 1988). *Apatania auricula* and *Limnephilus fuscinervis* are recorded from Ireland but not from Britain (O'Connor 1978; Wallace *et al.* 1985).

Family	Genus	Species
GLOSSOSOMATIDAE	GLOSSOSOMA Curtis, 1834	*boltoni* Curtis, 1834
		conformis Neboiss, 1963
		*intermedium (Klapálek, 1892)
	AGAPETUS Curtis, 1834	*delicatulus* McLachlan, 1884
		fuscipes Curtis, 1834
		ochripes Curtis, 1834
HYDROPTILIDAE	AGRAYLEA Curtis, 1834	*multipunctata* Curtis, 1834
		sexmaculata Curtis, 1834
	ALLOTRICHIA McLachlan, 1880	*pallicornis* (Eaton, 1873)
	HYDROPTILA Dalman, 1819	*angulata* Mosely, 1922
		cornuta Mosely, 1922
		forcipata (Eaton, 1873)
		*lotensis Mosely, 1930
		martini Marshall, 1977
		occulta (Eaton, 1873)
		pulchricornis Pictet, 1834
		simulans Mosely, 1920
		sparsa Curtis, 1834
		*sylvestris Morton, 1898
		tigurina Ris, 1894
		tineoides Dalman, 1819
		*valesiaca Schmid, 1947
		*vectis Curtis, 1834
	OXYETHIRA Eaton, 1873	**distinctella* McLachlan, 1880
		falcata Morton, 1893
		flavicornis (Pictet, 1834)
		frici Klapálek, 1891
		*mirabilis Morton, 1904
		sagittifera Ris, 1897
		simplex Ris, 1897
		tristella Klapálek, 1895
	TRICHOLEIOCHITON Kloet & Hincks, 1944	*fagesii* (Guinard, 1879)
	ITHYTRICHIA Eaton, 1873	*clavata* Morton, 1905
		lamellaris Eaton, 1873
	ORTHOTRICHIA Eaton, 1873	*angustella* (McLachlan, 1865)
		costalis (Curtis, 1834)
		*tragetti Mosely, 1930

Family	Genus	Species
PHRYGANEIDAE	AGRYPNIA Curtis, 1835	*crassicornis (McLachlan, 1876) (Agrypnetes crassicornis) obsoleta (Hagen, 1864) (Phryganea obsoleta) pagetana Curtis, 1835 *picta Kolenati, 1848 varia (Fabricius, 1793) (Phryganea varia)
	HAGENELLA Martynov, 1924	*clathrata (Kolenati, 1848) (Oligotricha clathrata)
	OLIGOTRICHA Rambur, 1842	striata (Linnaeus, 1758) (O. ruficrus)
	PHRYGANEA Linnaeus, 1758	bipunctata Retzius, 1783 (P. striata) grandis Linnaeus, 1758
	TRICHOSTEGIA Kolenati, 1848	*minor (Curtis, 1834)
BRACHYCENTRIDAE	BRACHYCENTRUS Curtis, 1834	*subnubilus Curtis, 1834
LEPIDOSTOMATIDAE	CRUNOECIA McLachlan, 1876	irrorata (Curtis, 1834)
	LASIOCEPHALA Costa, 1857	basalis (Kolenati, 1848)
	LEPIDOSTOMA Rambur, 1842	hirtum (Fabricius, 1775)
LIMNEPHILIDAE	IRONOQUIA Banks, 1916	*dubia (Stephens, 1837)
	APATANIA Kolenati, 1848	auricula (Forsslund, 1930) muliebris McLachlan, 1866 (nielseni Schmid, 1954)† wallengreni McLachlan, 1871
	DRUSUS Stephens, 1837	annulatus (Stephens, 1837)
	ECCLISOPTERYX Kolenati, 1848	guttulata (Pictet, 1834)
	ALLOGAMUS Schmid, 1955	*auricollis (Pictet, 1834)
	ENOICYLA Rambur, 1842	*pusilla (Burmeister, 1839)
	HALESUS Stephens, 1836	digitatus (Schrank, 1781) radiatus (Curtis, 1834)
	HYDATOPHYLAX Wallengren, 1891	infumatus (McLachlan, 1865)
	MELAMPOPHYLAX Schmid, 1955	*mucoreus (Hagen, 1861)
	MESOPHYLAX McLachlan, 1882	*aspersus (Rambur, 1842) impunctatus McLachlan, 1884
	MICROPTERNA Stein, 1874 (STENOPHYLAX)	lateralis (Stephens, 1837) sequax McLachlan, 1875
	POTAMOPHYLAX Wallengren, 1891	cingulatus (Stephens, 1837) latipennis (Curtis, 1834) *rotundipennis (Brauer, 1857)

† A. nielseni is now considered to be a form of A. muliebris (Barnard & O'Connor 1987).

Family	Genus	Species
	STENOPHYLAX Kolenati, 1848	permistus McLachlan, 1895
		*vibex (Curtis, 1834)
	CHAETOPTERYX Stephens, 1829	villosa (Fabricius, 1798)
	ANABOLIA Stephens, 1837	nervosa (Curtis, 1834)
	GLYPHOTAELIUS Stephens, 1837	pellucidus (Retzius, 1783)
	GRAMMOTAULIUS Kolenati, 1848	nigropunctatus (Retzius, 1783)
		(G. atomarius)
		*nitidus (Müller, 1764)
	LIMNEPHILUS Leach, 1815	affinis Curtis, 1834
		auricula Curtis, 1834
		binotatus Curtis, 1834
		*bipunctatus Curtis, 1834
		*borealis (Zetterstedt, 1840)
		centralis Curtis, 1834
		coenosus Curtis, 1834
		decipiens (Kolenati, 1848)
		elegans Curtis, 1834
		*extricatus McLachlan, 1865
		flavicornis (Fabricius, 1787)
		*fuscicornis (Rambur, 1842)
		fuscinervis (Zetterstedt, 1840)
		griseus (Linnaeus, 1758)
		hirsutus (Pictet, 1834)
		ignavus McLachlan, 1865
		incisus Curtis, 1834
		lunatus Curtis, 1834
		luridus Curtis, 1834
		marmoratus Curtis, 1834
		nigriceps (Zetterstedt, 1840)
		pati O'Connor, 1980
		*politus McLachlan, 1865
		rhombicus (Linnaeus, 1758)
		sparsus Curtis, 1834
		stigma Curtis, 1834
		*subcentralis (Brauer, 1857)
		*tauricus Schmid, 1964
		vittatus (Fabricius, 1798)
	NEMOTAULIUS Banks, 1906	*punctatolineatus (Retzius, 1783)
	PHACOPTERYX Kolenati, 1848	brevipennis (Curtis, 1834)
	RHADICOLEPTUS Wallengren, 1891	*alpestris (Kolenati, 1848)
GOERIDAE	GOERA Stephens, 1829	pilosa (Fabricius, 1775)
	SILO Curtis, 1833	nigricornis (Pictet, 1834)
		pallipes (Fabricius, 1781)

Family	Genus	Species
BERAEIDAE	BERAEA Stephens, 1833	*maurus* (Curtis, 1834)
		pullata (Curtis, 1834)
	BERAEODES Eaton, 1867	*minutus* (Linnaeus, 1761)
	ERNODES Wallengren, 1891	**articularis* (Pictet, 1834)
SERICOSTOMATIDAE	NOTIDOBIA Stephens, 1829	**ciliaris* (Linnaeus, 1761)
	SERICOSTOMA Latreille, 1825	*personatum* (Spence in Kirby & Spence, 1826)
ODONTOCERIDAE	ODONTOCERUM Leach, 1815	*albicorne* (Scopoli, 1763)
MOLANNIDAE	MOLANNA Curtis, 1834	*albicans* (Zetterstedt, 1840) (*M. palpata*)
		*angustata Curtis, 1834
LEPTOCERIDAE	ATHRIPSODES Billberg, 1820	*albifrons* (Linnaeus, 1758)
		aterrimus (Stephens, 1836)
		bilineatus (Linnaeus, 1758)
		cinereus (Curtis, 1834)
		commutatus (Rostock, 1874)
	CERACLEA Stephens, 1829 (ATHRIPSODES)	*albimacula* (Rambur, 1842) (*A. alboguttatus*)
		annulicornis (Stephens, 1836)
		dissimilis (Stephens, 1836)
		fulva (Rambur, 1842)
		nigronervosa (Retzius, 1783)
		senilis (Burmeister, 1839)
	LEPTOCERUS Leach, 1815	**interruptus* (Fabricius, 1775)
		*lusitanicus (McLachlan, 1884)
		*tineiformis Curtis, 1834
	MYSTACIDES Latreille, 1825	*azurea* (Linnaeus, 1761)
		longicornis (Linnaeus, 1758)
		*nigra (Linnaeus, 1758)
	ADICELLA McLachlan, 1877	**filicornis* (Pictet, 1834)
		reducta (McLachlan, 1865)
	EROTESIS McLachlan, 1877	**baltica* McLachlan, 1877
	TRIAENODES McLachlan, 1865	*bicolor* (Curtis, 1834)
	YLODES Milne, 1934 (TRIAENODES)	**conspersus* (Rambur, 1842)
		reuteri (McLachlan, 1880)
		*simulans (Tjeder, 1929)
	OECETIS McLachlan, 1877	*furva* (Rambur, 1842)
		lacustris (Pictet, 1834)
		notata (Rambur, 1842)
		ochracea (Curtis, 1825)
		testacea (Curtis, 1834)
	SETODES Rambur, 1842	*argentipunctellus* McLachlan, 1877
		*punctatus (Fabricius, 1793)

COLLECTION, PRESERVATION AND EXAMINATION

Collection. Case-bearing caddis larvae live in all types of waterbody except the most temporary or polluted. They are not restricted to the riffles and weed beds which can be sampled with a traditional pond net. They also occur on the roots of marginal vegetation and under large stones and are frequently encountered in small waterbodies such as inconspicuous trickles, shallow grassy marshes, ditches and pools which only hold water over winter, tiny pools between tussocks on bogs, sulphurous-smelling leaf-filled pools in woods and even in salt-marsh pools. These small waterbodies can be worked with aquarium nets but it is often more rewarding to explore them by hand, looking under pebbles and twigs and amongst plant material. One species, *Enoicyla pusilla*, is terrestrial.

The larvae of almost all species are at an identifiable instar at some time between March and May and this is a good time for a faunal survey. It is often worth while to collect pupal cases because, even if the pupa is immature or the adult has emerged, there is frequently enough of the larval exuviae (cast skin) to enable identification. Pupal cases should be transported dry so that sclerites are not washed out. They are often attached to stones, logs or other objects and may be easier to find than larvae.

Preservation. Larvae can be preserved in the field or transported alive in damp moss or in leaf litter taken from their habitat and drained of surplus water. They may leave their cases during either procedure. As the case is useful in identification it should not be discarded.

Animals used in preparing the keys were killed, fixed and preserved by immersion in a 70–80% solution of industrial methylated spirits in deionized water. Better fixatives exist, e.g. Kahle's and Pampel's fluids, but it is recommended that material should then be transferred to the alcohol solution because the fixatives may cause serious colour changes when used for long-term storage. They are also more toxic and pungent. Alcohol removes the colour of the fat-body but this feature is not used in the keys. Alcohol solutions easily weaken by evaporation; material is then likely to become soft and sclerites may darken. A slight darkening of the sclerites and fading of colour patterns seems to be inevitable after many years of storage, and considerable care may be needed when identifying specimens over ten years old. A larva and its case contain much water which weakens the alcohol solution, resulting in poor fixation. A change of alcohol after a few hours is therefore recommended. Specimens should be stored in darkness to prevent bleaching.

Preserved larvae are easily damaged by movement of the cases and identification labels when specimens are sent by post, so the tube's contents should be immobilized with cellulose wadding.

The legs consist of six elements (see Fig. 2); the coxa is proximal (nearest the body) and the tarsal claw is distal (furthest from the body). The trochanter and sometimes the femur, tibia and tarsus are subdivided, but they articulate as single elements. The labrum ('upper lip') and mandibles ('jaws') are retractable and may need to be pulled forward for examination.

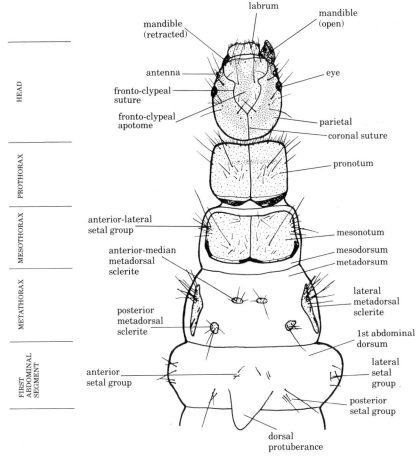

Fig. 1.   Typical cased caddis larva (*Limnephilus lunatus*): head, thorax and 1st abdominal segment, dorsal view.

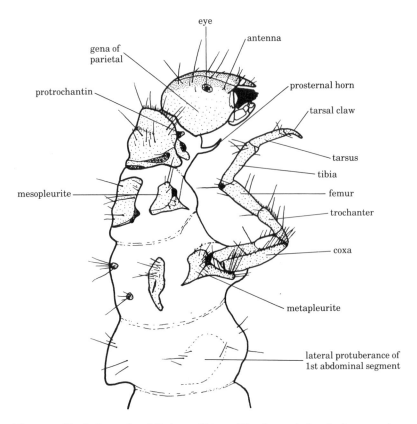

Fig. 2.   Typical cased caddis larva (*Limnephilus lunatus*): head, thorax and 1st
          abdominal segment, lateral view, (1st and 2nd legs omitted).

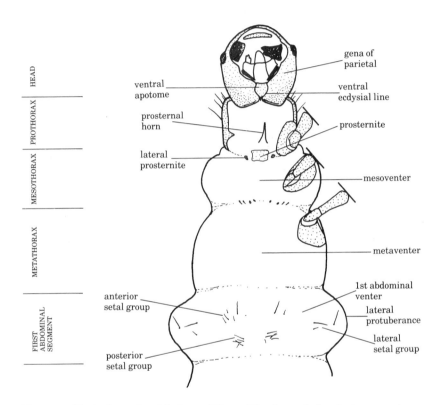

Fig. 3. Typical cased caddis larva (*Limnephilus lunatus*): head, thorax and 1st abdominal segment, ventral view, (legs omitted).

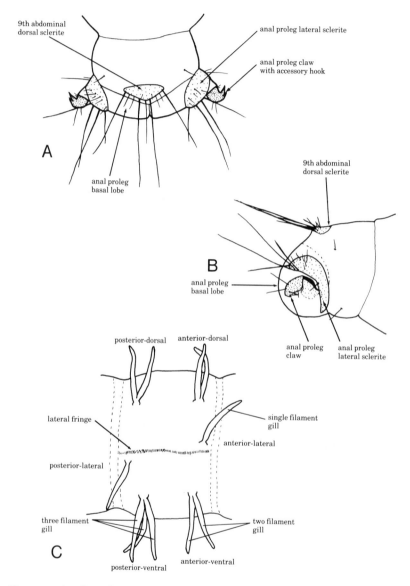

Fig. 4.   **A – C**: typical cased caddis larva (*Limnephilus lunatus*): A, 9th abdominal
segment, dorsal view; B, 9th abdominal segment, lateral view; C, 4th
abdominal segment, lateral view.

NOTES ON THE KEYS

Lay-out. Following an initial Key to Families, each family of case-bearing larvae is dealt with separately. Each Family Key is prefaced by a short introduction which users are urged to read carefully as it will enable them to check that they have arrived at the appropriate family. The introduction also gives general information on the biology of the family and draws attention to any features in the Key which may require particular care. After identification to species, there is an inset section (in smaller type) which gives additional features, such as head colour or a description of the case, and information on habitat and distribution.

Larvae hold their heads and legs at various angles to the body but for the purposes of the keys the following conventions are adopted. The head is described as though it were extended with the mouth directed anteriorly (forwards) so that the surface which includes the fronto-clypeal apotome (Fig. 1) is dorsal. The legs are described as if extended at right-angles to the body with their broad faces directed anteriorly and posteriorly and with narrow dorsal and ventral edges. Text-figures are aligned with the anterior to the top of the page in dorsal and ventral views and to the right in lateral views. The distal end of leg elements lies to the right of the page. Mouthparts are normally omitted from drawings of the head. The text-figures show final instar larvae unless otherwise stated.

Early instars. The great majority of caddis have five larval instars, each terminated by a moult. They are denoted instar I (first instar after hatching) to instar V (final larval instar before the moult to the pupa). Reported exceptions are *Sericostoma personatum* (at least six instars) and *Agapetus fuscipes* (seven instars). With successive moults there is a general tendency for colour and patterning of sclerites to become more distinct and for numbers of setae and gills to increase. Thus, many species can only be identified with confidence at the later instars.

In each Family section, the range of head widths (and number measured) is tabulated for different instars, based on British and Irish material. (Head width is the width of the head capsule at its widest point, excluding the eyes if they protrude beyond the outline of the head.) Unless otherwise stated, all instars for which head width measurements are given can be identified to species using the key.

At instar I, many family characteristics are absent or poorly developed and these larvae are not considered here.

Biology. Descriptions of habitat and distribution are based on our own observations, data abstracted from museum collections, the records of the Trichoptera Recording Scheme operated by I. D. Wallace for the Biological Records Centre of the Institute of Terrestrial Ecology and the records of J. P. O'Connor of the National Museum of Ireland, Dublin. When considering the habitat, it should be remembered that larvae may be carried by water movement into an atypical habitat and persist there for some time. A convention has been adopted for describing distribution: 'widespread' means that the species occurs throughout the British Isles, whilst 'throughout Britain' implies absence from Ireland.

Life cycles are outlined for each family to indicate when particular sizes of larvae are normally encountered. There is little published information on this (full life cycle data are available for only about 30 of the 152 species of case-bearing caddis) and we have relied heavily on our own observations. Life cycles may vary with location and the information given here should be taken only as a rough guide.

Sources of taxonomic information. Previously published keys form the basis of the present work. All have been revised to accommodate early instars, assist where difficulties are known to have existed in their use, and to achieve uniformity. A large number of specimens was examined during the course of the revision; most are now housed in Liverpool Museum.

Sources of information are as follows:–

General reference – Hickin (1967), Lepneva (1971), Nielsen (1942), Siltala (1907).

Key to families – Wiggins (1977), with additional information from Edington & Hildrew (1981) (whose key separates groups of families of case-bearing caddis from caseless families and is satisfactory though difficult to use with some early instar larvae and badly preserved material) and from Siltala (1907).

Beraeidae – Wiberg-Larsen (1979).

Brachycentridae – Only one species in the British Isles.

Glossosomatidae – Mackereth (1956).

Goeridae – Hiley (1972) with additional information from Nielsen (1942).

Hydroptilidae – Marshall (1978), Nielsen (1948) and Wiggins (1977) with additional information from Barnard (1971) and Giudicelli & Vaillant (1967).

Lepidostomatidae – Hiley (1972).

Leptoceridae – Wallace (1981) with additional information from Wallace (1976).

Limnephilidae – Hiley (1976) and Wallace (1980) with additional information from Botosaneanu (1974) on *M. aspersus*, Garside (1979), Wallace (1978), Wallace *et al.* (1985) and Wallace & Wallace (1985). G. B. Wiggins allowed us to use unpublished information about early instar *Ironoquia* and N. Williams suggested the fronto-clypeal apotome character for *Halesus* species. L. Botosaneanu donated larvae of *M. aspersus* from the Canary Islands.

Molannidae – Leader (1968).

Odontoceridae – Only one species in the British Isles.

Phryganeidae – Bray (1967) with additional information from Bray (1964), Gislason (1979) on *A. picta*, Solem (1971) and Wallace & Wiggins (1978). G. Gislason donated larvae of *A. picta* from Iceland.

Sericostomatidae – Wallace (1977).

KEY TO FAMILIES

1   Pronotum with 5 setae on each side (include the alveoli of detached setae but not the 2 pits, *p* in Fig. 5A, which are present at all instars); 1 of the 5 setae lies at the anterior-lateral corner and there are no other setae along the anterior edge (Figs 5A, B)— Instar I (first after hatching)

> Instar I is not considered further in this key; see Siltala 1907.

—   Pronotum with more than 5 setae on each side (some of which may be small and pale); more than 1 seta lies on the anterior edge (Figs 5C, 7E–H, 8F, G)—   **2**

2   Dorsum of each thoracic segment largely covered by sclerotized plates (Figs 5D, 6A–D)—   **3**

—   Metadorsum and sometimes mesodorsum entirely membranous or with widely spaced sclerites (e.g. Figs 7E–H, 8F, G)—   **5**

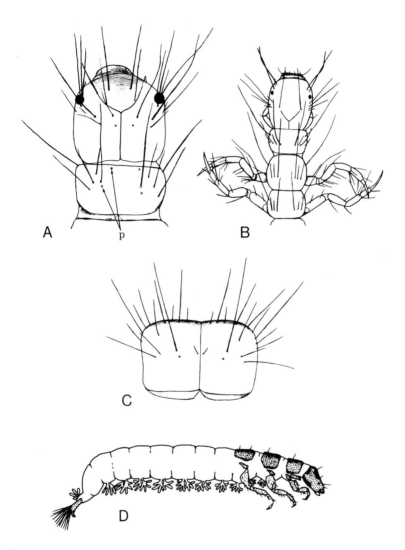

Fig. 5. **A**: head and pronotum, dorsal view, of *Nemotaulius punctatolineatus*, instar I. **B**: head and thorax, dorsal view, of *Plectrocnemia conspersa* (Curtis), instar I. **C**: pronotum, dorsal view, of *N. punctatolineatus*, instar II. **D**: typical larva of the family Hydropsychidae, lateral view.

3   Ventro-lateral gills, branched at instars III–V, on abdominal segments
    (Fig. 5D). Anal proleg with a terminal brush of long setae at instars
    III–V (Fig. 5D)—   Caseless: Family HYDROPSYCHIDAE
                                    (See Edington & Hildrew 1981)

—   No ventro-lateral gills on abdominal segments (Figs 6A, C). Anal
    proleg without a terminal brush of long setae (Figs 6A, C, D)—   4

4   9th abdominal dorsum with a sclerotized plate (arrow, Figs 6A, D,
    E)—   Family HYDROPTILIDAE (Figs 6A, B, D), p. 70

—   9th abdominal dorsum without a sclerotized plate (Figs 6C, F)—
                            Caseless: Family ECNOMIDAE
                                    (See Edington & Hildrew 1981)
    Prominent lateral fringe of setae on abdominal segments 2–8 (Fig.
    6C). Hydroptilidae instars II–IV, which are caseless, have prominent
    lateral setae but are further distinguished from Ecnomidae by the
    presence of sclerites on the dorsa of abdominal segments 1–8 (Fig.
    6D) and slender anal proleg claws which are not sharply angled
    distally (see Figs 6D, F).

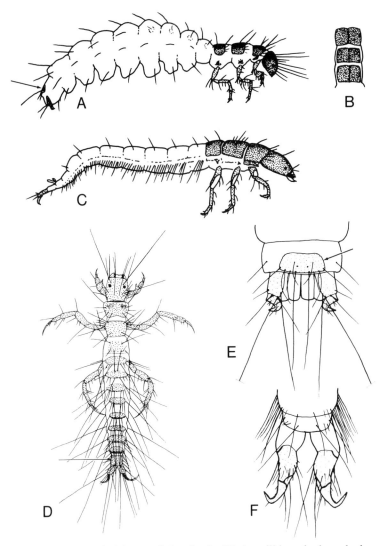

Fig. 6.   **A, B**: typical larva of the family Hydroptilidae: A, lateral view; B, dorsal sclerites of thorax.   **C**: *Ecnomus tenellus* (Rambur) (Ecnomidae), lateral view of larva.   **D, E**: *Agraylea multipunctata* (Hydroptilidae): D, dorsal view of instar III; E, 9th abdominal segment, dorsal view, instar V.   **F**: 9th abdominal segment, dorsal view, of *Ecnomus tenellus* (Ecnomidae).

5(2)Larva with ANY of the following features:
   (a) 1st abdominal segment with lateral and, usually, dorsal pro-
        tuberances (*pr* in Figs 10G, 11A, C); lateral protuberance may
        bear a sclerite *s* (Fig. 10G).
   (b) Anal proleg short and squat, with a transversely aligned lateral
        sclerite *s* (Figs 7A–D).
   (c) Metadorsum with more than 2 anterior-lateral setae (arrow, Figs
        7E-H)—   **8**

— Larva with ALL the following features:
   (a) 1st abdominal segment with neither lateral or dorsal protuber-
        ances nor a lateral sclerite (Figs 9A, B).
   (b) Anal proleg long and tapering, with a longitudinally aligned
        lateral sclerite *s* (Figs 8A–E).
   (c) Metadorsum with only 2 anterior-lateral setae (arrow, Figs 8F,
        G), one of which may be very small and pale—   **6**

Fig. 7. **A, B**: 9th abdominal segment of *Limnephilus lunatus* (Limnephilidae):
A, dorsal view; B, lateral view. **C, D**: 9th abdominal segment of
Phryganea bipunctata (Phryganeidae): C, dorsal view; D, lateral
view. **E–H**: thoracic segments, dorsal view: E, *Potamophylax lati-
pennis* (Limnephilidae); F, *Brachycentrus subnubilus* (Brachycentridae);
G, *Beraea maurus* (Beraeidae); H, *Phryganea bipunctata* (Phryganeidae).

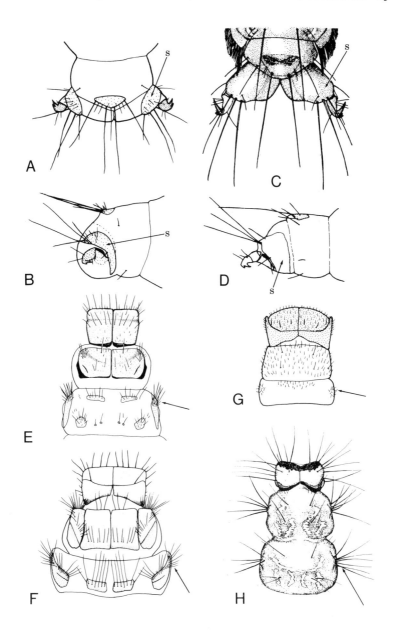

6   9th abdominal dorsum with sclerotized plate *n* (Figs 8B–D)—   7

—   9th abdominal dorsum without sclerotized plate (Figs 8A–E)—
                    Caseless: Families PHILOPOTAMIDAE,
            POLYCENTROPODIDAE, PSYCHOMYIIDAE
                          (See Edington & Hildrew 1981)

Fig. 8.   **A–E**: 9th abdominal segment: A, *Plectrocnemia conspersa* (Polycentropo-
            didae), dorsal view; B, *Rhyacophila dorsalis* (Curtis) (Rhyacophilidae),
            dorsal view; C, *Agapetus fuscipes* (Glossosomatidae), dorsal view; D,
            A. fuscipes, lateral view; E, *Tinodes waeneri* (Psychomyiidae), lateral
            view.   **F, G**: thoracic segments, dorsal view: F, *Plectrocnemia conspersa*
            (Polycentropodidae); G, *Agapetus fuscipes* (Glossosomatidae).

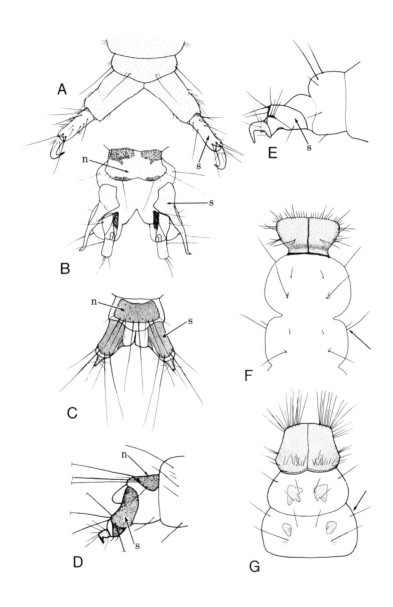

7   Branched gills present on abdominal segments (Fig. 9A). Prosternal
    plates absent—
                        Caseless: Family RHYACOPHILIDAE
                            (See Edington & Hildrew 1981)

—   No gills present on abdominal segments (Fig. 9B). Prosternal plates
    prominent (arrows, Fig. 9C)—
                        Family GLOSSOSOMATIDAE, p.52

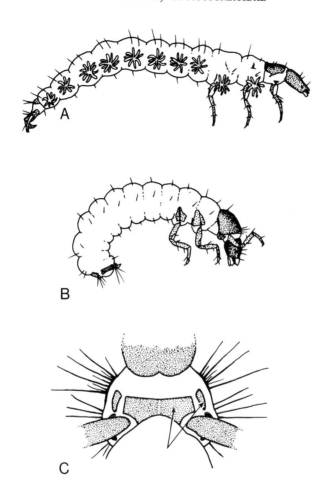

Fig. 9.   **A**: typical larva of the family Rhyacophilidae, lateral view.   **B**: typical larva of the family Glossosomatidae, lateral view.   **C**: prothorax, ventral view, of *Agapetus fuscipes* (Glossosomatidae).

8(5)EITHER: antenna long and slender (arrow, Fig. 10A), at least six
    times longer than its width at widest part (excluding terminal seta,
    length *l* in Fig. 10B), and always situated very close to anterior
    margin of head capsule; OR: mesonotum lightly pigmented except
    for a pair of dark, curved posterior-lateral projections (arrows, Fig.
    10F; projections may be hidden in the intersegmental fold). (Some
    species have both characters.)—
                    Family LEPTOCERIDAE (Figs 10G, H), p. 84
                    and *Beraeodes minutus* (Beraeidae), p. 42

—   Antenna not long and slender (arrow, Figs 10C–E), at most four
    times longer than its width at widest part (excluding terminal seta),
    sometimes situated some distance behind anterior margin of head
    capsule (arrow, Figs 10D, 13A, C, D) AND mesonotum (if present)
    without curved posterior-lateral projections—   **9**

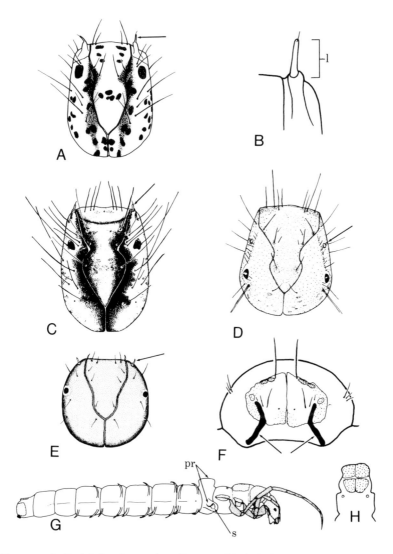

Fig. 10.   **A, B**: *Athripsodes aterrimus* (Leptoceridae): A, head capsule; B, anterior-lateral region of head capsule.   **C–E**: head capsule: C, *Molanna angustata* (Molannidae); D, *Goera pilosa* (Goeridae); E, *Beraea pullata* (Beraeidae).   **F**: mesodorsum of *Ceraclea albimacula* (Leptoceridae).   **G, H**: typical larva of the family Leptoceridae: G, lateral view; H, dorsal sclerites of thorax.

9   Mesodorsum and metadorsum largely unsclerotized (though they may
    be pigmented) and very similar to each other in both setal arrangement
    and colouration (Fig. 7H)—
                        Family PHRYGANEIDAE (Figs 11A, B), p. 214

—   Mesodorsum largely covered by sclerotized plates (which may lack
    colour, particularly in small larvae) and different from the metador-
    sum in setal arrangement and often also in colour (Figs 7E–G)—   **10**

10 Mesopleurite with an anterior process *ap* which projects free from
    body wall (Figs 11C, D)—   Family GOERIDAE, p. 66

—   Mesopleurite without an anterior process which projects free from
    body wall—   **11**

11 Tibia of *1st* leg with a ventral process (arrow, Fig. 11E) terminating
    in a strong seta. Tarsal claw of 3rd leg with several fine spines in
    addition to the basal seta *b* (Fig. 11G)—
                        Family MOLANNIDAE (Figs 11H, I), p. 208

—   Tibia of *1st* leg without a ventral process (Fig. 11F). Tarsal claw of
    3rd leg with only the basal seta *b* (as in Fig. 11F)—   **12**

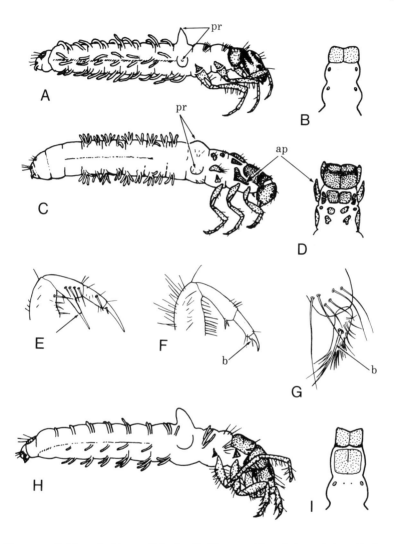

Fig. 11. **A, B**: typical larva of the family Phryganeidae: A, lateral view; B, dorsal
sclerites of thorax. **C, D**: typical larva of the family Goeridae: C,
lateral view; D, dorsal sclerites of thorax. **E, F**: tibia and tarsus of 1st
leg, posterior view: E, *Molanna angustata* (Molannidae); F, *Odontocerum
albicorne* (Odontoceridae). **G**: tarsal claw of 3rd leg, posterior view,
of *M. angustata* (Molannidae). **H, I**: typical larva of the family Molannidae: H, lateral view; I, dorsal sclerites of thorax.

12   Tibiae of *2nd and 3rd* legs each with a ventral process (arrow, Figs
     12A, B) terminating in a strong seta. Metadorsum with sclerites and
     their associated setal groups arranged in a transverse curve (Figs
     7F, 12C, E). 1st abdominal segment with neither lateral nor dorsal
     protuberances—
                    Family BRACHYCENTRIDAE (Figs 12D, E), p. 48

—   Tibiae of *2nd and 3rd* legs and metadorsum not as above. 1st abdominal
     segment with lateral and (except in Lepidostomatidae) dorsal pro-
     tuberances—   **13**

13   Anal proleg with a ventral brush of setae *b* just below the claw *c* (Fig.
     12H) and with a dorsal process (arrow, Fig. 12G) bearing setae, one
     of which is very much longer and stouter than the others. Pronotum
     with a flap-like anterior-lateral corner which (except in some larvae
     with a head width less than 0·3 mm) extends forwards as a lobe *l* and
     from which a sharp ridge runs obliquely backwards (Figs 12I, J)—
                              Family BERAEIDAE, p. 42
                    except *Beraeodes minutus* (See couplet 8, above)

—   Anal proleg with neither a brush of setae just below the claw *c* (Fig.
     12F) nor a dorsal process. Pronotum with neither a flap-like anterior-
     lateral corner nor a sharp ridge, though the corner may be sharply
     angled or produced into a point—   **14**

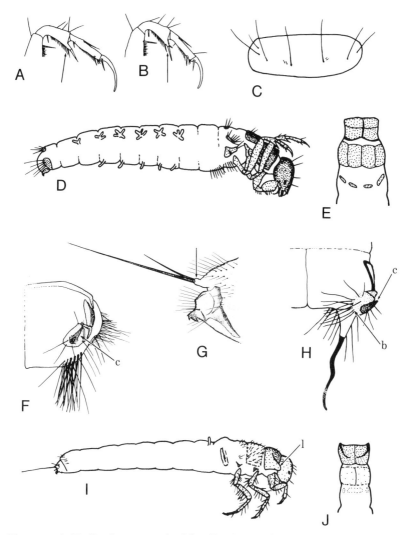

Fig. 12. **A–E**: *Brachycentrus subnubilus* (Brachycentridae): A, tibia and tarsus of 2nd leg; B, tibia and tarsus of 3rd leg; C, metadorsum, instar II; D, larva, lateral view; E, dorsal sclerites of thorax. **F–H**: 9th abdominal segment: F, *Sericostoma personatum* (Sericostomatidae), left side, ventral view; G, *Beraea maurus* (Beraeidae), lateral view; H, *Ernodes articularis* (Beraeidae), left side, ventral view. **I, J**: typical larva of the family Beraeidae: I, lateral view; J, dorsal sclerites of thorax.

14 Antenna (arrow, Figs 13A, C, D) situated some distance behind
    anterior margin of head capsule. Prosternal horn present (arrow, Fig.
    13F). Anterior-lateral corner of pronotum never sharply angled or
    produced to a point (Figs 13F, G)—   **15**

—   Antenna (arrow, Fig. 14I) situated very close to anterior margin
    of head capsule. Prosternal horn absent. Anterior-lateral corner of
    pronotum may be sharply angled or produced to a point (Figs 15G,
    I)—   **16**

15 1st abdominal segment with a dorsal protuberance (arrow, Fig. 13G;
    this may have collapsed but will be visible as a wrinkle in dorsal
    view, arrow, Fig. 13H). Antenna (arrow, Fig. 13A) at least as close
    to anterior margin of head capsule as to eye (except in the terrestrial
    Enoicyla pusilla). Gena without a fold alongside the ventral apotome
    (Fig. 13B)—
                    Family LIMNEPHILIDAE (Figs 13G, H), p. 127

—   1st abdominal segment without a dorsal protuberance (Figs 13I, J).
    Antenna (arrow, Figs 13C, D) situated very close to anterior margin
    of the eye. Gena with a fold *f* (Fig. 13E) alongside the ventral apotome
    (this fold is not always obvious in pale larvae)—
                    Family LEPIDOSTOMATIDAE (Figs 13I, J), p. 80

Fig. 13.   **A, B**: head capsule of *Limnephilus auricula* (Limnephilidae): A, dorsal
           view; B, ventral view.   **C–E**: *Lepidostoma hirtum* (Lepidostomatidae):
           C, left eye and antenna; D, head capsule; E, ventral apotome and
           adjoining areas of genae.   **F–H**: typical larva of the family Limnephili-
           dae: F, head and thorax, lateral view, 1st leg omitted to show prosternal
           horn; G, larva, lateral view; H, dorsal sclerites of thorax and protuber-
           ances of 1st abdominal segment.   **I, J**: typical larva of the family
           Lepidostomatidae: I, lateral view; J, dorsal sclerites of thorax and
           protuberances of 1st abdominal segment.

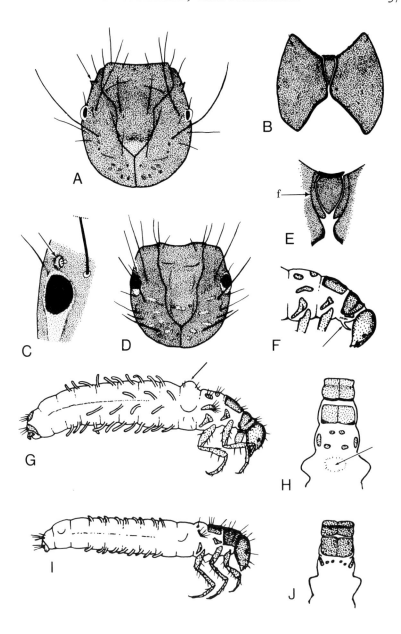

16(14) Anal proleg claw with accessory hooks and a sharply angled crook
(Figs 14A–D). Anal proleg with more than 5 setae *ds* on the dorsum
(Figs 14A, B) except when the head width is less than 0·25 mm.
Protrochantin *pt* large with a hook-shaped tip (Figs 15A–C). (Fronto-
clypeal apotome dark brown except in some larvae with a head width
less than 0·5 mm, never with an anchor-shaped mark)—
        Family SERICOSTOMATIDAE (Figs 15G, H), p. 227

— Anal proleg claw without accessory hooks and with a gently curved
crook (Figs 14E–H). Anal proleg never with more than 5 setae *ds* on
the dorsum (Figs 14E, F). Protrochantin *pt* small, without a hook-
shaped tip (Figs 15D–F). (Fronto-clypeal apotome pale with a distinct
anchor-shaped mark, Fig. 14I, except in larvae with a head width less
than 0·9 mm.)—
        Family ODONTOCERIDAE (Figs 15I, J), p. 212

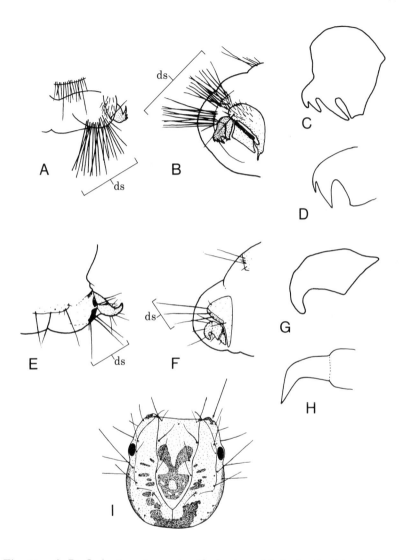

Fig. 14. **A–D**: *Sericostoma personatum* (Sericostomatidae): A, 9th abdominal segment, right side, dorsal view; B, 9th abdominal segment, lateral view; C, anal proleg claw; D, anal proleg claw, instar ?II. **E–I**: *Odontocerum albicorne* (Odontoceridae): E, 9th abdominal segment, right side, dorsal view; F, 9th abdominal segment, lateral view; G, anal proleg claw; H, anal proleg claw, instar II; I, head capsule.

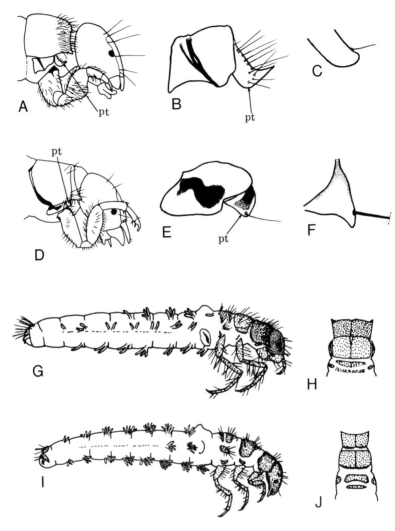

Fig. 15. **A–C**: *Sericostoma personatum* (Sericostomatidae): A, head and prothorax, lateral view; B, propleurites; C, protrochantin, instar ?II. **D–F**: *Odontocerum albicorne* (Odontoceridae): D, head and prothorax, lateral view; E, propleurites; F, protrochantin, instar II. **G, H**: typical larva of the family Sericostomatidae: G, lateral view; H, dorsal sclerites of thorax. **I, J**: *Odontocerum albicorne* (Odontoceridae): I, larva, lateral view; J, dorsal sclerites of thorax.

KEYS TO SPECIES

Family BERAEIDAE

Four species occur in the family Beraeidae (Table 1). The larvae are found amongst moss and dead leaves in springs, and amidst dense vegetation and roots in flowing marshes and at the edges of streams and rivers. They are small, with curved tapering cases, up to 1 cm long, which are made of sand grains (Figs 16C, 18D, E).

Two of the three genera, *Beraea* and *Ernodes*, have striking orange or brick-coloured heads and share several distinctive characters. The pronotum has a sharp ridge marking off the flap-like anterior-lateral corner which (except in instar II *Beraea*) extends forwards as a lobe (Figs 16E, F). The anal proleg has a posteriorly directed dorsal process bearing setae, one of which is much longer and stouter than the others (Figs 17D–F). In ventral view the anal proleg claw has a brush of dark setae arising from a membranous area at its base (*b*, Fig. 17B). Other cased caddis larvae have only five setae around the claw and another three pale setae below the point (as in Fig. 12F). Very young sericostomatids have pale brown heads and superficially resemble *Beraea* and *Ernodes*, but the anal proleg lacks all three features described above. *Sericostoma personatum* is occasionally found with *Beraea*. (Certain microscopical characters of the larvae suggest an affinity between Beraeidae and Sericostomatidae, most notably the peculiar form of the lateral line which is illustrated by Denis (1984).)

The third genus, *Beraeodes*, lacks many of the features which characterize other beraeids; it resembles leptocerids in its slender appearance, long antennae and third pair of legs (Figs 16A, C). The mosaic pattern on the pronotum, at least at the final instar (Fig. 16B), and the numerous setae on the fronto-clypeal apotome (Fig. 35G) readily distinguish this larva from the leptocerids.

The flight period of beraeids is quite short, from early to mid summer, but final instar larvae of *Beraea* and *Ernodes* can be found during most of the year. It seems likely that some species require more than one year for the life cycle; half-grown larvae of *E. articularis* have been found during the adult flight period. Wiggins (1977) reported a similar observation for the North American *Beraea fontana* Wiggins.

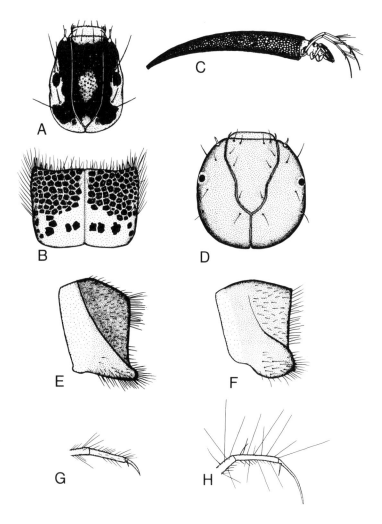

Fig. 16.   **A–C**: *Beraeodes minutus:* A, head capsule; B, pronotum; C, larva in case.   **D**: head capsule of *Beraea pullata*.   **E, F**: pronotum, lateral view: E, *Ernodes articularis*; F, *Beraea pullata*.   **G, H**: tarsus and claw of 3rd leg, posterior view: G, *Ernodes articularis;* H, *B. pullata.*

TABLE I. HEAD WIDTHS OF BERAEIDAE
Ranges (and *n*) of head widths (mm) at instars II to V.

Species	Instar			
	II	III	IV	V
Beraea maurus	—	0·34–0·43 (4)	0·52–0·55 (3)	0·59–0·74 (16)
B. pullata	0·18–0·27 (7)	0·43 (1)	—	0·83–0·90 (6)
Beraeodes minutus	—	—	0·32–0·42 (3)	0·51–0·59 (18)
Ernodes articularis	0·24 (1)	0·31–0·41 (7)	0·56 (1)	0·72–0·79 (5)

Key to larvae

1 Head with extensive black areas (Fig. 16A). Pronotum with a black mosaic pattern (Fig. 16B), (less conspicuous at early instars than at instar V). Anal proleg with neither a ventral brush of dark setae below the claw (Fig. 17A) nor any dorsal seta which is very much longer and stouter than the others (Fig. 17C)—   **Beraeodes minutus** (L.)

> Associated with submerged roots of emergent vegetation, e.g. tree roots, in shallow water at the edges of rivers, streams and lakes. Widespread.

— Head without extensive black areas, uniformly straw to red-brown in colour (Fig. 16D). Pronotum without a black mosaic pattern, similar in colour to the head (Figs 16E, F). Anal proleg with a ventral brush of dark setae *b* below the claw *c* (Fig. 17B) and one dorsal seta which is very much longer and stouter than the others (Figs 17D–F)—   **2**

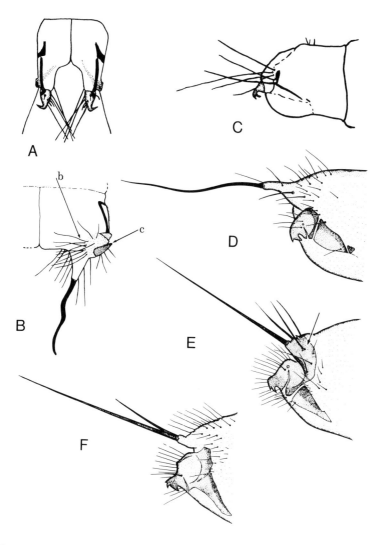

Fig. 17. **A, B**: 9th abdominal segment, ventral view: A, *Beraeodes minutus;* B, *Ernodes articularis*. **C–F**: 9th abdominal segment, lateral view: C, *B. minutus;* D, *E. articularis;* E, *Beraea pullata;* F, *Beraea maurus*.

2 Posterior end of case with a hemispherical prominence on which the opening is situated ventrally (Figs 18D, F). Pronotum with a bluntly pointed anterior-lateral corner (which extends forwards as a lobe at instars II–V, Fig. 16E). Anal proleg claw with 1 erect accessory hook (arrow, Fig. 18A)— **Ernodes articularis** (Pictet)

> Head reddish-brown at instars IV and V, straw-coloured at instars II and III. 3rd leg with tarsus longer than claw at instars IV and V (Fig. 16G), similar in length at instars II and III. Longest seta of anal proleg dorsal process is black and sinuous (Figs 17B, D).

> Among moss and fallen leaves in small springs and trickles of hard water, especially where travertine is depositing. Rare; Clwyd and scattered sites in southern England. *Beraea maurus* is often found with it.

— Posterior end of case without a hemispherical prominence (Figs 18E, G). Pronotum with a broadly rounded anterior-lateral corner (which extends forwards as a lobe at instars III–V, Fig. 16F, head width more than 0·3 mm). Anal proleg claw with EITHER 2 erect accessory hooks OR 1 decumbent accessory hook (arrows, Figs 18B, C)— **3**

> Head orange or reddish-orange at instars IV and V, straw-coloured at instars II and III. 3rd leg with tarsus about as long as claw at instar V (Fig. 16H), shorter than claw at instars II–IV. Longest seta of anal proleg dorsal process is orange to dark brown and straight (Figs 17E, F); (the seta may be distorted in preserved material, particularly in prepupae and recently moulted specimens).

3 Anal proleg claw with 1 decumbent accessory hook (arrow, Fig. 18B). Anal proleg dorsal process with three setae which are about one-third as long as the largest seta (Fig. 17E); (there are also some very small dorsal setae which are never numerous)— **Beraea pullata** (Curtis)

> Anal proleg dorsal process with a brownish sclerite at instars IV and V (arrow, Fig. 17E).

> Among dense vegetation in flowing marshes, springs and at the edges of streams. Widespread and common.

— Anal proleg claw with 2 erect accessory hooks (arrows, Fig. 18C). Anal proleg dorsal process with one seta which is about half as long as the largest seta (Fig. 17F); (there are also some very small setae which are numerous at instar V)— **Beraea maurus** (Curtis)

> Anal proleg dorsal process without an obvious sclerite at any instar (Fig. 17F).

> Among moss and fallen leaves in small springs and trickles, often with *Crunoecia irrorata*. Widespread and common.

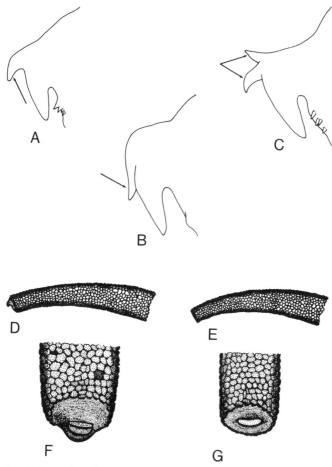

Fig. 18. **A–C**: anal proleg claw and accessory hook(s): A, *Ernodes articularis*; B, *Beraea pullata*; C, *B. maurus*. **D, E**: case, lateral view: D, *E. articularis*; E, *B. pullata*. **F, G**: posterior end of case, ventral view: F, *E. articularis*; G, *B. pullata*.

Family BRACHYCENTRIDAE

The only British representative of this family is *Brachycentrus subnubilus* Curtis (Table 2). It is widely distributed in rivers and large streams, where it is often present in considerable numbers. The species has not been recorded from Ireland.

The case of the full-grown larva is tubular and composed almost entirely of secretion, though this has an uneven texture and appearance due particularly to the presence of small pieces of plant material embedded within it (Fig. 19A). At early instars the case is rectangular in section and constructed of transversely arranged plant material held together by secretion (Fig. 19B); it is rather like the case of final instar *Lepidostoma hirtum*.

Brachycentrus subnubilus can be recognized by the presence, on the tibiae of the *second* and *third* legs, of a disto-ventral process terminating in a strong seta (Figs 12A, B). The pronotum has a curved transverse ridge which is visible from instar II as a thin line on the dorsum (Fig. 12E). At instars IV and V the mesonotum is clearly divided into four sclerites and the metadorsum has four sclerites arranged in a transverse curve (Fig. 12E); at earlier instars the sclerites are pale and difficult to see but the position of those on the metadorsum is indicated by their associated setae (Fig. 12C). Anterior metadorsal sclerites and setae are absent at all instars. The first abdominal segment differs from that of most other cased caddis larvae in lacking dorsal and lateral protuberances. At later instars, the head has a distinctive pattern (Fig. 19C).

The larvae of *B. subnubilus* have a method of feeding which is unlike that used by any other British caddis. The case is attached to a substratum, such as a weed stem or a tree root, in flowing water with its anterior end facing into the current (Fig. 19D). The long second and third legs are extended outwards (as in Figs 19E, F) and, by virtue of the fine spines on their femora, form a filter mechanism which captures particles from the water stream. Murphy (1919), working with the North American species *B. nigrisoma* Banks which is morphologically similar to *B. subnubilus*, has described in detail how material so caught is removed and transferred to the mouth by the first legs, which also are also provided with fine spines. Larger particles and organisms, including copepods, cladocerans and hydracarines, are seized between the second and third legs assisted by their long claws and tibial spines, and devoured. It is probable that the

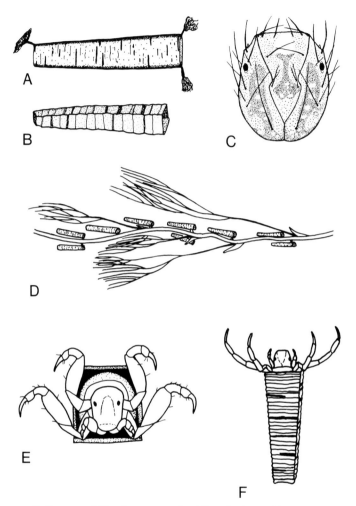

Fig. 19. **A–B**: case of *Brachycentrus subnubilus*: A, instar V; B, instar III. **C**: head of *B. subnubilus*. **D**: several cases of *B. subnubilus* attached to *Ranunculus* weed. **E–F**: feeding attitude of *B. nigrisoma*: E, anterior view; F, dorsal view.

long setae of the thorax and first abdominal segment prevent the case from becoming clogged by water-borne debris. If this is abundant, the larva will partially withdraw from its case and clean off material adhering to the anterior segments. Casual observations by one of us (IDW) indicate similar behaviour by *B. subnubilus*. The larvae can also detach their cases and move to a new site when there is an adverse change in current.

The adult flight period is in spring. Larvae appear soon afterwards and some reach the final instar by late autumn. Growth seems to continue over winter.

TABLE 2.   HEAD WIDTHS OF BRACHYCENTRIDAE
Ranges (and *n*) of head widths (mm) at instars II to V of *Brachycentrus subnubilus*.

Instar		
II	III	*IV, V
0·25–0·31 (5)	0·36–0·47 (4)	0·67–1·19 (86)

*Larvae with head widths in this range could not be reliably separated into instars.

Family GLOSSOSOMATIDAE

The family Glossosomatidae is closely related to families which have caseless larvae. This relationship is reflected in features such as the elongate form of the anal proleg lateral sclerite (*s* in Fig. 20G) and absence of protuberances on the first abdominal segment. The mandibles lack large teeth (Figs 20A, B) and the larvae feed on organisms and fine detritus scraped from surfaces.

The characteristic cases (Figs 20C, D) are abundant and conspicuous on stones in streams and rivers. Both openings of the case are alike and the larva regularly reverses its position. *Agapetus* cases differ from those of *Glossosoma* in having a loose collar of sand grains at each opening (Figs 20E, F) which collapses when the larva retreats, closing the entrance. Glossosomatid cases are not continuously enlarged as in other case-bearing families; each instar builds a larger case, attached to one end of the existing case, then bites off the old one (Anderson & Bourne 1974). For pupation the larva cuts away the underside of the case and fixes the rim of the upper dome to a stone. A brown cocoon is constructed inside this shelter. *Glossosoma* pupal shelters are 9 to 12 mm long while those of *Agapetus* range from 5 to 7 mm (exceptionally 3·5 to 9 mm in *A. fuscipes*).

Glossosoma boltoni, *G. conformis* and the three *Agapetus* species are widespread. In some stony rivers it is possible to find all five in the same sample. Adults have been collected from spring to autumn, but large larvae are most numerous in spring. There may be more than one generation a year. The rare *G. intermedium* has a short spring flight period and overwinters as a full-grown larva in a pupal cocoon. (*G. boltoni* and *A. fuscipes* can also be found in this state during winter, so the habit is by no means diagnostic.)

Nielsen (1942) recorded seven larval instars in Danish *A. fuscipes* but Anderson & Bourne (1974) found only five head width groups in the North American *A. bifidus* Denning. It is not known how many instars are undergone by *Agapetus* species in the British Isles; hence the instars are denoted final, final − 1 and final − 2 in Table 3. *Glossosoma* appears to have the usual five larval instars; the authors have found five distinct head width groups, including instar I.

Separation of the two genera is straightforward. Separation of the species is more difficult and the following points should be read before tackling the key.

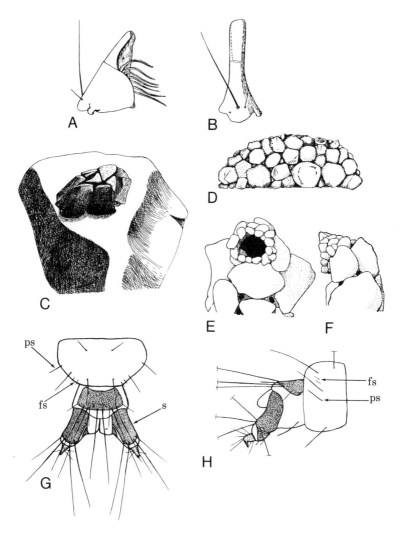

Fig. 20. **A, B**: right mandible of *Agapetus fuscipes*: A, ventral view; B, lateral view. **C**: pupal case of *Glossosoma intermedium* attached to a stone. **D–F**: larval case of *A. fuscipes*: D, lateral view; E, ventral view of opening; F, lateral view of opening. **G, H**: 8th and 9th abdominal segments of *A. fuscipes*: G, dorsal view; H, lateral view.

Pronotal characters.   The pronotum has a small area of thickening where it abuts the coxa and this is associated with a very darkly pigmented mark (*m*, Figs 23F, 25A). The extent of the mark (which is larger than the thickened area) is useful in identifying all six species. It is important not to confuse the mark *m* with the darkly coloured pleurite *pe* or proximal tip of the coxa *c* which in some poses lie just under the edge of the pronotum and are visible through it (Figs 23F, 25A). In *Agapetus* the pronotum in the vicinity of the mark may be deeper brown than most of the rest of the sclerite but only the region which is as dark as the band associated with the posterior pronotal groove (*b* in Figs 25A–C) is regarded as constituting the mark. In *Glossosoma* neither the mark nor the characters concerning the posterior pronotal band can be used with recently moulted specimens as typical colouration takes some time to develop. Such specimens may be recognized by the presence of a very small lateral mark which does not incorporate the outer seta *os* (see Figs 23F–H for position of the outer seta).

Eighth abdominal segment.   The posterior-lateral seta *ps* of the eighth abdominal segment is inconspicuous in some species and relatively prominent in others. The setae on the segment are best viewed from behind (Figs 24A–C). Seta *ps* is easily detached by rough treatment, for example during collection by kick sampling, and may be missing, especially if any of the six large dorsal setae show evidence of damage.

Tarsal claw.   The form of the basal seta of the tarsal claw is useful in separating the *Agapetus* species. Just after a moult, all three species have setae with tapering flexuous tips. *Agapetus fuscipes* usually retains this form (Fig. 24E) whilst in *A. ochripes* the flexuous tip wears away quickly, though the residual part of the seta may be curved (Fig. 24D). (Wear in *A. delicatulus* is very variable.) All *Agapetus* species may be found with severely worn setae and claws (as in Fig. 24F) and the character should not be used in such larvae.

TABLE 3. HEAD WIDTHS OF GLOSSOSOMATIDAE
Ranges (and *n*) of head widths (mm) at various instars.

Species	Instar		
	Final −2	Final −1	Final
Agapetus			
delicatulus	*0·23–0·25 (10)	0·32–0·40 (30)	0·46–0·52 (40)
A. fuscipes	*0·27–0·30 (25)	0·32–0·43 (50)	†0·47–0·54 (50)
A. ochripes	*0·19–0·20 (3)	*0·25–0·28 (15)	0·36–0·45 (50)

	II	III	IV	V
Glossosoma				
boltoni	*0·19–0·22 (3)	*0·29–0·31 (5)	0·42–0·52 (25)	0·61–0·72 (25)
G. conformis	*0·20–0·22 (4)	*0·31–0·34 (6)	0·50–0·53 (10)	0·66–0·77 (15)
G. intermedium	—	*0·34 (1)	0·50–0·53 (6)	0·63–0·72 (12)

*Not keyed to species at this instar.

†*A. fuscipes* is very variable in size. Some final instar larvae (from very small mountain streams) had the same head width as penultimate instar larvae from lowland sites and are not included in the table.

Key to larvae

1   Each side of pronotum with up to 7 setae along anterior margin (Fig.
    21A). Mesodorsum and metadorsum without median sclerites. Basal
    seta of tarsal claw arises from a prominence (arrow, Figs 21D, E).
    Gena with a line (arrow, Fig. 21G) alongside median ventral ecdysial
    line (Fig. 21G)—   Genus GLOSSOSOMA, 2

        Glossosoma species are not separable at instars II and III: head width
        less than 0·4 mm.

—   Each side of pronotum with more than 7 setae along anterior margin
    (Fig. 21B), (except in some larvae of head width less than 0·15 mm).
    Mesodorsum and metadorsum with median sclerites (arrows, Fig.
    21C); (sclerites may not be apparent in larvae of head width less than
    0·25 mm). Basal seta of tarsal claw does not arise from a prominence
    (Figs 21F, 24D–F). Gena without a line alongside median ventral
    ecdysial line (Fig. 21H)—   Genus AGAPETUS, 4

        Agapetus species are not separable when head width is less than 0·3
        mm.

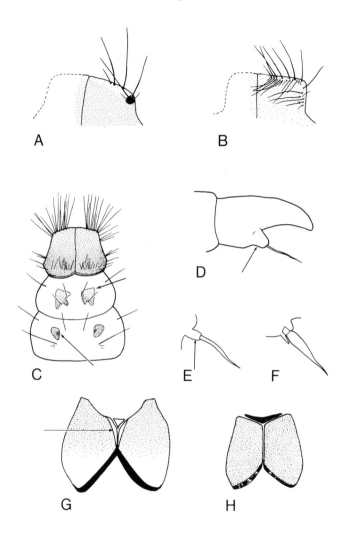

Fig. 21. **A, B**: pronotum, anterior part of right half: A, *Glossosoma boltoni*; B, *Agapetus fuscipes*. **C**: thorax of *A. fuscipes*, dorsal view. **D**: tarsal claw of *G. conformis*. **E, F**: basal seta of tarsal claw: E, *G. conformis*, instar II; F, *A. delicatulus*. **G, H**: head capsule, ventral view: G, *G. boltoni*; H, *A. delicatulus*.

2   9th abdominal dorsal sclerite with outermost setae (arrows, Fig. 22A)
    much shorter and thinner than the six large intermediate setae—
                              Glossosoma intermedium (Klapálek)
                                                      Instars IV and V

> Fronto-clypeal apotome with lateral bulge (arrow, Fig. 22C). Dark
> lateral mark of pronotum narrow, extending inwards about half way
> between outer seta *os* and inner seta *is* (Fig. 23G). On the pronotum,
> the black band *b* associated with the posterior groove fades completely
> or narrows considerably towards the median suture; the area posterior
> to the band in region *R* is usually darker than the opposing area
> anterior to the band (Fig. 23C). 8th abdominal segment with post-
> erior-lateral seta *ps* pale, not normally visible, smaller than the small
> fine dorsal setae *fs* (as in Fig. 22E).
>
> Rare; the only recent records are from two small streams in the
> English Lake District.

—   9th abdominal dorsal sclerite with outermost setae (arrows, Fig. 22B)
    similar in length and thickness to the six large intermediate setae—
                                                                        3

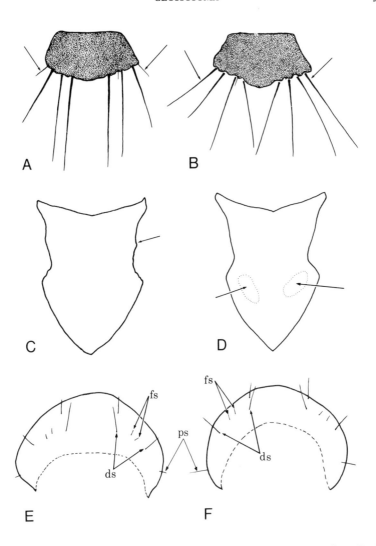

Fig. 22. **A, B**: 9th abdominal dorsal sclerite: A, *Glossosoma intermedium*; B, *G. boltoni*. **C, D**: fronto-clypeal apotome: C, *G. intermedium*; D, *G. boltoni*. **E, F**: 8th abdominal segment, posterior-dorsal view: E, *G. conformis*; F, *G. boltoni*.

3   8th abdominal segment with posterior-lateral seta *ps* inconspicuous,
    paler than the large dorsal setae *ds* and rarely longer than the small,
    fine dorsal setae *fs* (Fig. 22E). Region *R* of posterior margin of
    pronotum either entirely black (Fig. 23A) or with any brown pigment
    posterior to the dark band *b*, associated with the posterior groove,
    darker than pigment of opposing area anterior to the band (Fig. 23B);
    the band usually extends to the median suture (Figs 23A, B)—

    Glossosoma conformis Neboiss
    Instars IV and V

    Dark lateral mark of pronotum frequently extends further inwards
    than inner seta *is* and usually shades into the general colour of the
    sclerite (Fig. 23H). Posterior part of fronto-clypeal apotome without
    pale areas.

    Stony substratum in streams and rivers. Widespread and common in
    northern and western Britain, rare elsewhere.

—   8th abdominal segment with posterior-lateral seta *ps* as dark as the
    large dorsal setae *ds* and usually longer than the small, fine dorsal
    setae *fs* (Fig. 22F). Region *R* of posterior margin of pronotum never
    entirely black and with any brown pigment posterior to the dark band
    b, associated with the posterior groove, similar in shade to pigment
    of opposing area anterior to the band (Figs 23D, E); the band usually
    fades completely or narrows considerably towards the median suture
    (Figs 23D, E)—   **Glossosoma boltoni** Curtis
    Instars IV and V

    Dark lateral mark of pronotum rarely extends further inwards than
    inner seta *is* and usually has a distinct edge, not shading into the
    general colour of the sclerite (Fig. 23F). Posterior part of fronto-
    clypeal apotome may have two pale areas (arrows, Fig. 22D).

    Stony substratum in large streams and rivers. Widespread and com-
    mon in northern and western Britain and in Ireland.

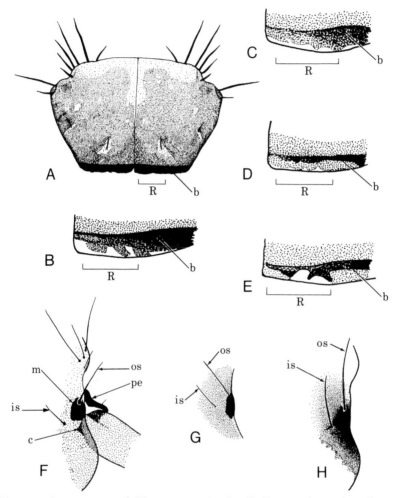

Fig. 23. **A**: pronotum of *Glossosoma conformis*. **B–E**: posterior region of pronotum, area of right side adjacent to median suture: B, *G. conformis*; C, *G. intermedium*; D, E, *G. boltoni*. **F**: prothorax in region of articulation of pronotum with leg, dorso-lateral view, of *G. boltoni*. **G, H**: pronotum in region of articulation with leg, dorso-lateral view: G, *G. intermedium*; H, *G. conformis*.

4(1)8th abdominal segment with posterior-lateral seta *ps* dark and conspicuous, larger than the small fine dorsal setae *fs* (Figs 20G, H,
24A)—   **Agapetus fuscipes** Curtis
                                                        Last two instars

> Most specimens key out here. For additional features see the second
> parts of couplets 5 and 6.

> Stony substratum; permanent streams of all sizes, rivers and lake
> shores. Widespread and abundant.

—   8th abdominal segment with posterior-lateral seta *ps* pale and inconspicuous, similar in size to or smaller than the fine dorsal setae *fs*
(Figs 24B, C)—   5

5   On the pronotum, that portion of the lateral mark *m* which is as dark
as the posterior band *b*, extends more than half way between setal
group *a* and seta *p* (Fig. 25A). Metadorsal sclerite *ts* has a maximum
dimension which is less than half the distance between metadorsal
setae *ta* and *tp* and less than the distance between mesodorsal setae *sa*
and *sp* (Fig. 25D)—   **Agapetus delicatulus** McLachlan
                                                        Last two instars

> 8th abdominal segment with posterior-lateral seta *ps* pale and similar
> in size to the small, fine dorsal setae *fs* (Fig. 24B).

> Stony substratum in large streams and rivers. Northern and western
> Britain and southern half of Ireland; common.

—   On the pronotum, that portion of the lateral mark *m* which is as dark
as the posterior band *b* extends less than half way between setal group
a and seta *p* (Figs 25 B, C). Metadorsal sclerite *ts* has a maximum
dimension which is at least half the distance between metadorsal setae
ta and *tp* and at least as great as the distance between mesodorsal setae
sa and *sp* (Figs 25E, F)—   6

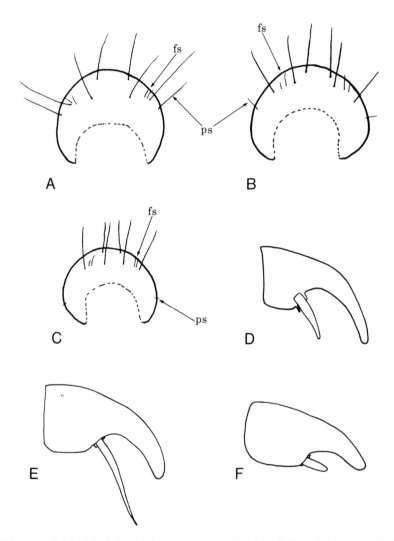

Fig. 24. **A–C**: 8th abdominal segment, posterior-dorsal view: A, *Agapetus fuscipes*; B, *A. delicatulus*; C, *A. ochripes*. **D–F**: tarsal claw: D, *A. ochripes*; E, *A. fuscipes*; F, *A. fuscipes* (severely worn).

6 Metadorsal sclerite *ts* has a maximum dimension which is about half
   the distance between metadorsal setae *ta* and *tp* and similar to the
   distance between mesodorsal setae *sa* and *sp* (Fig. 25E). Basal seta of
   tarsal claw without tapering flexuous tip, though it may be curved
   (Fig. 24D), (except in very recently moulted specimens)—

   Agapetus ochripes Curtis

   Final instar

   8th abdominal segment with posterior-lateral seta *ps* minute, not
   easily seen, much smaller than the fine dorsal setae *fs* (Fig. 24C).

   Stony substratum; rivers, also streams in southern England. Widespread and common.

— Metadorsal sclerite *ts* has a maximum dimension which is more than
   half (usually two-thirds) the distance between metadorsal setae *ta* and
   tp and much greater than the distance between mesodorsal setae *sa*
   and *sp* (Fig. 25F). Basal seta of tarsal claw with tapering flexuous tip
   (Fig. 24E), (unless claw is severely worn, as in Fig. 24F)—

   Agapetus fuscipes Curtis

   Last two instars

   Specimens with missing or damaged posterior-lateral setae on the 8th
   abdominal segment key out here.

   See couplet 4 for habitat and distribution.

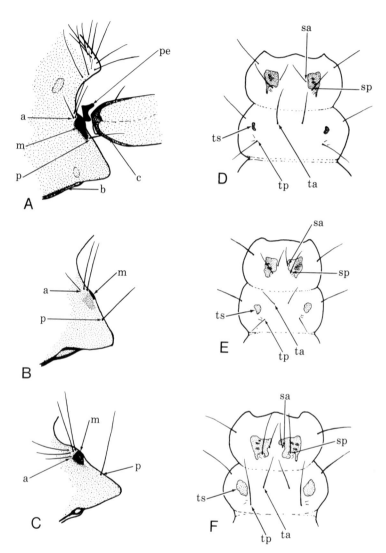

Fig. 25. **A**: prothorax in region of articulation of pronotum with leg, dorso-lateral view, of *Agapetus delicatulus*. **B, C**: pronotum in region of articulation with leg, dorso-lateral view: B, *A. ochripes*; C, *A. fuscipes*. **D–F**: mesodorsum and metadorsum: D, *A. delicatulus*: E, *A. ochripes*; F, *A. fuscipes*.

Family GOERIDAE

Larvae of the three goerid species (Table 4) are easily recognized by their characteristic mesopleurite, which is produced anteriorly as a finger-like process (*ap* in Figs 26C–F) projecting free from the body and extending forwards below the ventral edge of the pronotum. The anterior-lateral corners of the pronotum are also produced as pointed, forwardly-directed processes (Fig. 27E). Anteriorly, the head narrows markedly and has a distinctly humped appearance when viewed from the side.

The rigid, well-ballasted cases of the Goeridae are characteristic, consisting of a strong tube of sand grains with larger rock fragments incorporated laterally (Fig. 26A). When the larva retracts into its case the head and sclerites of the first and second thoracic segments form a domed plug which effectively seals off the anterior opening of the case, as described and figured by Nielsen (1942). Larvae feed by scraping algae and other materials from surfaces; they have plain, toothless tips to the mandibles (resembling Figs 56C, E) typical of this feeding method. Goerid larvae are particularly likely to be covered with a fine layer of sediment; this needs to be removed if it obscures important features.

The larvae are subject to parasitism by the ichneumon *Agriotypus armatus* Curtis, and it is not uncommon in some localities to find a pupal case with a long ribbon-like thread projecting from it (Fig. 26B). This is an extension of the cocoon of the contained parasite and is probably respiratory in function.

The flight period of all three goerids found in the British Isles extends from May to September. Final instar larvae can be found at most seasons but are commonest in spring and early summer.

TABLE 4. HEAD WIDTHS OF GOERIDAE
Ranges (and n) of head widths (mm) at instars II to V.

Species	Instar			
	II	III	IV	V
Goera pilosa	0·29–0·32 (6)	0·48, 0·57 (2)	0·71–0·86 (4)	1·08–1·24 (15)
Silo nigricornis†	*0·31–0·33	0·48–0·52	0·72–0·83	1·00–1·16
S. pallipes	*0·29 (1)	0·41–0·47 (7)	0·63–0·77 (38)	0·90–1·08 (13)

*Not keyed to species at this instar.
†Data from foreign material (Nielsen 1942)

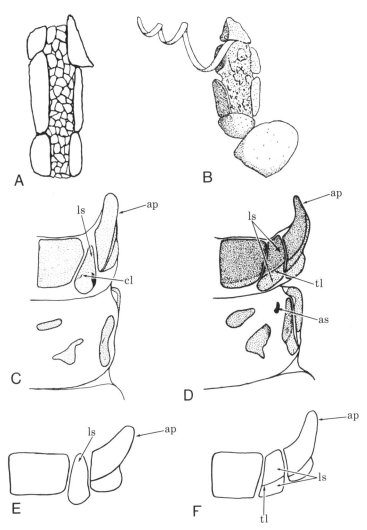

Fig. 26. **A**: case of *Silo pallipes*, dorsal view. **B**: pupal case of *Silo* sp.
parasitized by *Agriotypus armatus*. **C, D**: mesothorax and metathorax,
right half, dorsal view: C, *Goera pilosa*; D, *S. nigricornis*. **E, F**: outlines
of sclerites of mesothorax, right half, dorsal view: E, *G. pilosa*, instar
II; F, *S. pallipes*, instar II.

Key to larvae

1   Mesonotal lateral sclerite *ls* with bluntly pointed apex (Figs 26C, E); the sclerite is not divided into two by a transverse ecdysial line (though a curved brown line, *cl* in Fig. 26C, may mark off the polished posterior part of the sclerite from the remainder). Metadorsum without anterior-lateral sclerite (Fig. 26C). Fronto-clypeal apotome with bulbous posterior region (Fig. 27A)—   **Goera pilosa** (Fabricius)

> In fast-flowing water in streams and rivers and on gravelly lake shores. Widespread and common.

—   Mesonotal lateral sclerite *ls* with truncate apex (Figs 26D, F); sclerite is divided into two by a transverse ecdysial line *tl*★ (Figs 26D, F). Metadorsum with anterior-lateral sclerite *as*★ (Fig. 26D). Fronto-clypeal apotome with tapering posterior region (Fig. 27B)—

Genus SILO, 2

> (*Silo* species; asterisks denote characters that are not visible in some instar II larvae (head width less than 0·38 mm).)

2   Head width more than 0·38 mm—   **3**

—   Head width less than 0·38 mm—   **Silo nigricornis** (Pictet)
Silo pallipes (Fabricius)
Instar II

3   Posterior face of femur of 1st leg with additional setae *fs* on the proximal half (Fig. 27C). If head width is more than 0·60 mm, pronotum has 3 slightly raised areas (arrows, Fig. 27E) which are pale in contrast to the dark colour of the rest of the pronotum—
Silo pallipes (Fabricius)
Instars III to V

> Streams and rivers. Widespread and common.

—   Posterior face of femur of 1st leg without additional setae *fs* on the proximal half (though they are usually present on the distal half, Fig. 27D). Pronotum never with 3 pale areas, generally uniform in colour (Fig. 27F) or with a contrasting pale anterior margin in dark larvae—
Silo nigricornis (Pictet)
Instars III to V

> Streams and rivers. Common in south-east England, increasingly rarer further north; also recorded from Ireland.

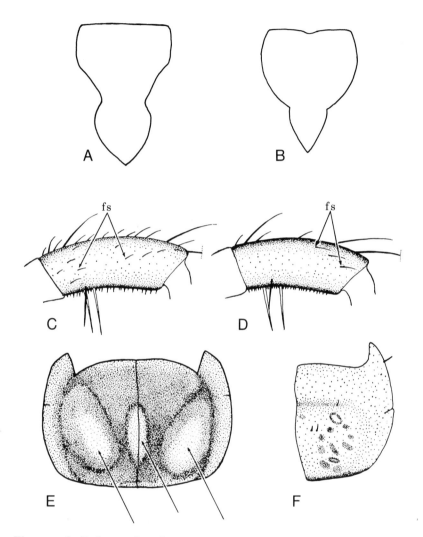

Fig. 27. **A, B**: fronto-clypeal apotome: A, *Goera pilosa*; B, *Silo nigricornis*. **C, D**: femur of 1st leg, posterior view: C, *S. pallipes*; D, *S. nigricornis*. **E**: pronotum of *S. pallipes*. **F**: pronotum, right half, of *S. nigricornis*.

Family HYDROPTILIDAE

Larvae of the family Hydroptilidae are very small, only 2·5 – 7·5 mm in length when fully grown. They are most likely to be encountered at the final instar (V), when the larva inhabits a distinctive, seed-like case (e.g. Figs 28E, 29A, 31D, 32B) which, in most genera, is strongly flattened laterally. At this stage the thoracic and 9th abdominal segments each bear a dorsal sclerotized plate.

The first four larval instars are caseless and differ markedly in form from the final instar. The anal proleg claws are long and slender and dorsal sclerites are present on the thoracic and all the abdominal segments. Setae, and gills if present, are relatively long. On assuming the final instar, the dorsal sclerites are lost from abdominal segments 1 to 8, the conspicuous lateral fringe of setae is lost from the abdomen, there are changes in the proportions of the larva, and case building commences. The enlargement of the abdomen during the final instar is very striking.

Found in all types of waterbody except small pools and temporary waters, the larvae feed on periphyton and fine organic particles. Some are specialized for feeding on filamentous algae (Wiggins 1977), the mouthparts being adapted for breaching the cell walls and sucking out the semi-fluid contents (Nielsen 1948). Disney (1972) has described larvae of *Orthotrichia* sp. sucking out the contents of pupae and eggs of *Simulium* Latreille in streams in Cameroon. Some species have two generations a year, overwintering as larvae or prepupae and flying in early summer; the offspring of this flight grow rapidly and adults appear from late summer.

Of the 31 known species of Hydroptilidae in Britain and Ireland, the larvae of only 20 have been described. The main published sources of information for these 20 species are listed below; asterisks denote sources that include information on the early instars.

Agraylea multipunctata: Nielsen (1948)*; Hickin (1967); Lepneva (1970); Solem (1972).
A. sexmaculata: Lepneva (1970); Barnard (1971); Solem (1972).
Allotrichia pallicornis: Giudicelli and Vaillant (1967).
Hydroptila forcipata: Fahy (1971)
H. lotensis: Kachalova (1972), crude figure only.
H. pulchricornis: Lepneva (1970).
H. sparsa: Hanna (1961); Hickin (1967); Lepneva (1970).
H. tineoides: Nielsen (1948)*; Hickin (1967); Lepneva (1970).
H. vectis: Jacquemart and Coineau (1962); Lepneva (1970).
Ithytrichia ?clavata: Ross (1944); Wiggins (1977).
I. lamellaris: Nielsen (1948)*; Hickin (1967); Lepneva (1970).
Orthotrichia angustella: Jacquemart (1962).

O. costalis: Nielsen (1948)*; Hickin (1967); Lepneva (1970).
Oxyethira distinctella: Lepneva (1970).
O. flavicornis: Nielsen (1948)*; Hickin (1967); Lepneva (1970).
O. frici: Lepneva (1970).
O. sagittifera: Siltala (1907)*; Lepneva (1970).
O. simplex: Macdonald (1950); Hickin (1967).
O. tristella: Lepneva (1970).
Tricholeiochiton fagesii: Lepneva (1970).

As a consequence of the variable detail of descriptions given in the above sources, and the lack of any information on the larvae of eleven species, only four species (Table 5) can be identified with confidence. However, described generic characters appear to be constant enough to allow identification to that level. Some features are most easily seen when the whole animal is mounted on a cavity slide and examined at a magnification of ×100. In most genera, the cases of well-grown final instar larvae are so distinctive and characteristic that the larvae can be identified to genus by the case alone.

TABLE 5. HEAD WIDTHS OF HYDROPTILIDAE
Ranges of head widths (mm) at instar V.

Species	Instar V
Agraylea multipunctata†	0·31–0·38
A. sexmaculata	0·25–0·28
Allotrichia pallicornis	0·32–0·38
Hydroptila tineoides†	0·19–0·23
Ithytrichia lamellaris†	0·27–0·33
Orthotrichia costalis†	0·21–0·24
Oxyethira flavicornis†	0·19–0·23
Tricholeiochiton fagesii	0·18

*British species that can be identified at instar V.
†Data from foreign material (Nielsen 1948)

Key to larvae

1   Anal proleg claw long and slender, not sharply angled (Figs 28A, B). Abdominal segments 1–8 with dorsal sclerites (Fig. 28A). Larva caseless—   Instars II to IV

      These early instars are not separated here, but further information is given by Siltala (1907) and by Nielsen (1948) who also provides a key to all genera except *Allotrichia* and *Tricholeiochiton*.

—   Anal proleg claw short and thick, sharply angled (Figs 28C, 32A). Abdominal segments 1–8 without dorsal sclerites (Figs 29E, F). Larva case-bearing—   **2**

2   Most abdominal segments with dorsal and ventral ovoid processes (Fig. 28D)—   Genus ITHYTRICHIA

      Case of secretion, oval in shape with a narrow anterior opening (Fig. 28E). Tibia of 1st leg without a ventral process (Fig. 28F), (unlike that of *Oxyethira*, a genus with a rather similar case; its ventral process is shown arrowed in Fig. 28G).

—   Abdominal segments without dorsal and ventral ovoid processes (e.g. Figs 29D, 30C, 31A)—   **3**

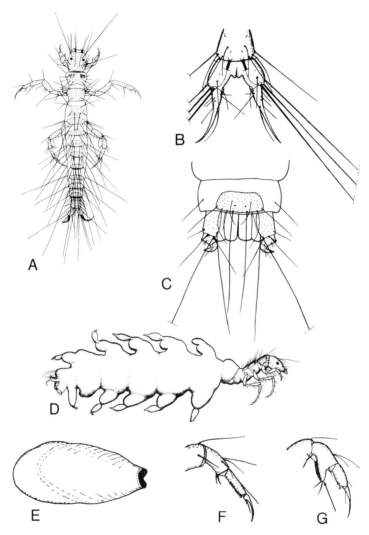

Fig. 28.   **A**: instar III larva of *Agraylea multipunctata*, dorsal view.   **B, C**: 9th abdominal segment, dorsal view, of *A. multipunctata*: B, instar IV; C, instar V.   **D, E**: *Ithytrichia lamellaris*: D, larva, lateral view; E, case, lateral view.   **F, G**: tibia and tarsus of 1st leg: F, *I. lamellaris*; G, *Oxyethira* sp.

3   Case not laterally compressed; there are two conspicuous ridges on
    each side of the mid-dorsal line (Figs 29A, B); case of secretion only.
    2nd abdominal segment with lateral protuberances which extend
    anteriorly alongside the 1st abdominal segment (arrow, Fig. 29E).
    Labrum with a median sclerotized point (arrow, Fig. 29C); (it is
    usually necessary to detach the labrum in order to distinguish the
    point clearly from other mouthparts)—   Genus ORTHOTRICHIA

    > Abdomen with neither deep intersegmental constrictions nor folds
    > across the segments (Figs 29D, E). Anal proleg claw without access-
    > ory hooks on its convex face (as in Fig. 32A). 2nd and 3rd legs up to
    > one-and-a-half times as long as 1st leg (Fig. 29D).

—   Case laterally compressed (Figs 30D, E; 31D, E), without ridges on
    each side of the mid-dorsal line; case of minute mineral particles
    or of secretion with or without incorporated algal filaments. 2nd
    abdominal segment without lateral protuberances and not extending
    anteriorly alongside the 1st abdominal segment (Fig. 29F). Labrum
    without a median sclerotized point (Figs 32E, F)—   4

4   2nd and 3rd legs at least twice as long as 1st leg (Figs 30A, C).
    Abdominal segments without transverse folds (Figs 30A, C). Case
    of secretion only, without incorporated algal filaments or mineral
    particles (Figs 30B, D)—   5

—   2nd and 3rd legs up to one-and-a-half times as long as 1st leg (Figs
    31A, 32C). Abdomen with transverse folds f across some segments
    (Figs 31A, 32C). Case of minute mineral particles or of secretion with
    incorporated algal filaments which may be transparent (Figs 31D,
    32B)—   6

5   2nd and 3rd legs 4–5 times as long as 1st leg (Fig. 30A). Tibiae of
    2nd and 3rd legs about twice as long as their respective tarsi (Fig.
    30A). Case with anterior and posterior ends of similar shape (Fig.
    30B)—   Genus TRICHOLEIOCHITON

    > **Tricholeiochiton fagesii** (Guinard) is the only species recorded in
    > the British Isles.
    >
    > Weedy, still waters. Rare.

—   2nd and 3rd legs 2–3 times as long as 1st leg (Fig. 30C). Tibiae of
    2nd and 3rd legs similar in length to their respective tarsi (Fig. 30C).
    Case with narrow anterior and broad posterior openings(Fig. 30D)—
                                              Genus OXYETHIRA

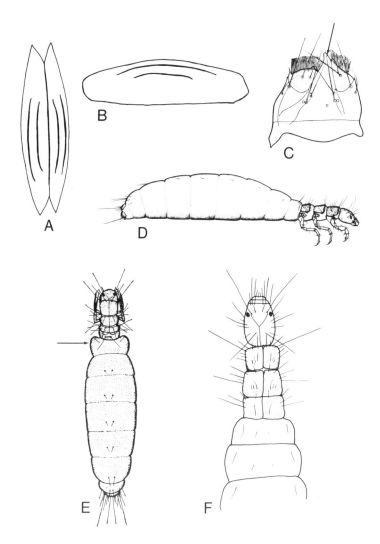

Fig. 29. **A, B**: case of *Orthotrichia costalis*: A, dorsal view; B, lateral view. **C**: labrum, dorsal view, of *O. costalis*. **D, E**: larva of *O. costalis*: D, lateral view; E, dorsal view. **F**: anterior part of larva of *Agraylea multipunctata*, dorsal view.

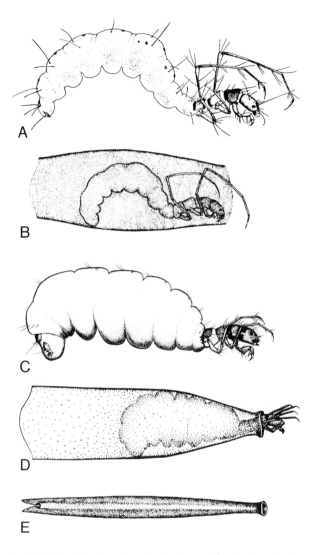

Fig. 30. **A, B**: *Tricholeiochiton fagesii*: A, larva, lateral view; B, larva in case, lateral view. **C–E**: *Oxyethira* sp.: C, larva, lateral view; D, larva in case, lateral view; E, case, ventral view.

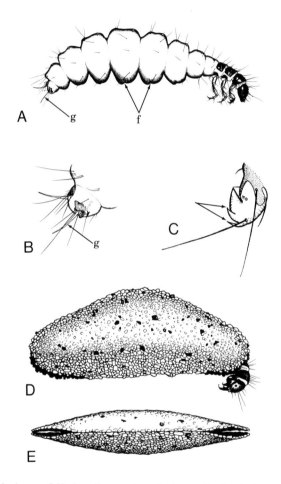

Fig. 31. **A**: larva of *Hydroptila* sp., lateral view. **B, C**: *Hydroptila tineoides*: B, 9th abdominal segment, lateral view; C, left anal proleg claw, median view. **D, E**: *Hydroptila* sp.: D, larva in case, lateral view; E, case, ventral view.

6(4) Anal proleg with gill filament *g* (Figs 31A, B). Anal proleg claw with accessory hooks (arrows, Fig. 31C). Case of sand grains (Figs 31D, E)—   Genus **HYDROPTILA**

— Anal proleg without gill filament. Anal proleg claw without accessory hooks (Fig. 32A). Case of secretion with incorporated algal filaments which may be transparent (Fig. 32B)—   **7**

7 Mesonotum and metanotum with dark markings (Figs 29F, 32D). Labrum with some very long setae (Fig. 32E). Tarsi of 2nd and 3rd legs about twice as long as tarsus of 1st leg (Figs 32G–I). Tibiae of 2nd and 3rd legs without a ventral prominence (Figs 32H, I). In still or slow-flowing water—   Genus **AGRAYLEA**

> Two species of *Agraylea* are recorded from the British Isles. **Agraylea sexmaculata** Curtis has a characteristic pattern of spots on the dorsal surface of the head and on the pro-, meso- and metanotum (Fig. 32D); **Agraylea multipunctata** Curtis lacks dark spots but has a posterior band of colour on the mesonotum and metanotum and sometimes also on the head and pronotum (Figs 29F, 32C).
>
> Both species occur in a wide variety of waterbodies. *A. multipunctata* is widespread and common; *A. sexmaculata* is less frequent.

— Mesonotum and metanotum uniformly pale, without dark markings. Labrum with short setae only (Fig. 32F). Tarsi of 2nd and 3rd legs similar in length to tarsus of 1st leg (Figs 32J–L). Tibiae of 2nd and 3rd legs each with a ventral prominence (arrows, Figs 32K, L). In fast-flowing water—   Genus **ALLOTRICHIA**

> **Allotrichia pallicornis** (Eaton) is the only species recorded in the British Isles.
>
> Streams and small rivers; stony substratum. Widespread, locally common.

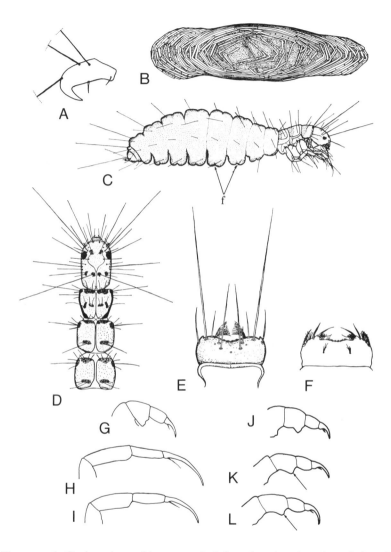

Fig. 32. **A–C**: *Agraylea multipunctata*: A, left anal proleg claw, lateral view; B, case, lateral view; C, larva, lateral view. **D**: head and thorax, dorsal view, of *Agraylea sexmaculata*. **E, F**: labrum, dorsal view: E, *A. multipunctata*; F, *Allotrichia pallicornis*. **G–I**: tibia and tarsus of *A. multipunctata*: G, 1st leg; H, 2nd leg; I, 3rd leg. **J–L**: tibia and tarsus of *A. pallicornis*: J, 1st leg; K, 2nd leg; L, 3rd leg.

Family LEPIDOSTOMATIDAE

There are only three species (Table 6) in the British Isles. All are found in permanent, flowing water and one, *Lepidostoma hirtum*, also occurs on lake shores. The larvae are small to medium in size and have brown heads, often with paler muscle attachment spots (Fig. 13D). They are distinguished from all other caddis larvae except the limnephilids by the arrangement of the dorsal sclerites of the thorax (Fig. 33A). Lepidostomatids differ from limnephilids by having a genal fold (*f*, Fig. 13E), by the position of the antennae, and by the absence of a dorsal protuberance on the first abdominal segment.

Early instar larvae of all three species construct cases of sand grains and these remain the constructional medium for all *Lasiocephala basalis* and some larvae of the other two species. Usually, however, *Crunoecia irrorata* and *L. hirtum* change to plant material for case-building, arranging it to give a square cross-section and producing a two-part case of a type unique to this family (Fig. 33D). Eventually, some larvae end up with a case composed entirely of plant material (Fig. 33E), which resembles that of young *Brachycentrus subnubilus* (Fig. 19B), the only other caddis to make a square-section case of plant material. *Lepidostoma hirtum* and *B. subnubilus* are often found together but the highly specialized legs of *B. subnubilus* easily distinguish it.

Final instar larvae can be found for many months of the year as all three species have fairly long summer flight periods. *Crunoecia irrorata* and *L. hirtum* have been found over winter at instars II–V, *L. basalis* at instars IV and V. Larvae of *L. basalis* aggregate for pupation (Jenkins 1974).

TABLE 6.   HEAD WIDTHS OF LEPIDOSTOMATIDAE
Ranges (and *n*) of head widths (mm) at instars II to V.

Species	Instar			
	II	III	IV	V
Crunoecia irrorata	0·22 (2)	0·29–0·32 (7)	0·43–0·51 (26)	0·61–0·70 (20)
Lasiocephala basalis	*0·25–0·26 (13)	0·37–0·43 (22)	0·61–0·70 (30)	0·99–1·15 (34)
Lepidostoma hirtum	*0·20–0·25 (10)	0·32–0·38 (32)	0·54–0·61 (14)	0·84–1·01 (13)

*Not keyed to species at this instar.

Key to larvae

1 Posterior metadorsal sclerite *p* with 1 seta, resembling the anterior-median sclerite *a*, which also bears a single seta (Figs 33A, C); (sclerites may be very pale in colour)— 2

— Posterior metadorsal sclerite *p* with more than 1 seta (1 large and 2 small at instar II, at least 6 at instar V), unlike the anterior-median sclerite *a* which bears a single seta (Fig. 33B)—
Crunoecia irrorata (Curtis)

Case initially circular in section, straight, made of sand grains; later, the larva usually changes to plant material for case construction, producing a case which is in part or entirely quadrangular in section (Fig. 33D).

Amongst dead leaves in shallow water of permanent trickles and oozes and at the margins of tiny woodland streams. Widespread and common.

2 Each side of mesonotum with several setae *as* on the anterior edge (3 to 4 at instar III, many at instar V) in addition to the anterior-lateral group (Fig. 33C)— **Lasiocephala basalis** (Kolenati)
Instars III to V

Case curved, made of sand grains (Fig. 33F).

In a variety of flowing waters. Widespread but local in England, Wales and Ireland, rare in Scotland; often abundant where found.

— Each side of mesonotum with only 1 seta *as* on the anterior edge in addition to the anterior-lateral group (Fig. 33A)— 3

3 Head width more than 0·3 mm— **Lepidostoma hirtum** (Fabricius)
                                              Instars III to V

   Case initially of sand grains, but by instar V it is usually composed
   mainly or entirely of plant fragments arranged to give a square cross-
   section (as in Figs 33D, E); occasionally, a larva does not change
   construction material and the instar V sand grain case may be slightly
   curved.

   Rivers, large streams and sometimes on lake shores. Widespread and
   common.

— Head width less than 0·3 mm— **Lasiocephala basalis** (Kolenati)
                                    Lepidostoma hirtum (Fabricius)
                                              Instar II

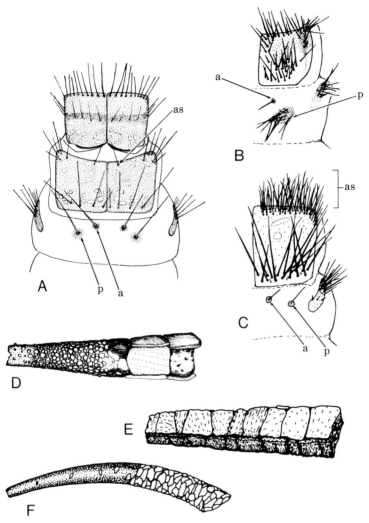

Fig. 33. **A**: thorax of *Lepidostoma hirtum*. **B, C**: mesodorsum and metadorsum, sclerites of right half: B, *Crunoecia irrorata*; C, *Lasiocephala basalis*. **D–F**: case: D, *C. irrorata*; E. *L. hirtum*; F, *L. basalis*.

Family LEPTOCERIDAE

Leptocerids are principally caddis of large waterbodies such as rivers and lakes. Final instar larvae of most species are found for only a short period, usually during early and mid summer; they are small, most being 6–12mm in length with head widths of 0·5–1·0 mm when full-grown (Table 7). There are 31 species in the British Isles and the larvae show a considerable degree of morphological variation.

Compared with other cased caddis, most leptocerid larvae have very long antennae. The exceptions are late instar sponge-eating *Ceraclea* larvae, which have short antennae protected by a lobe (Figs 43H, I) and are distinguished from larvae of other families by the presence of dark posterior-lateral projections on the mesonotum. Final instar leptocerids are characterized by the presence of an additional cleavage line on the head capsule, the subocular ecdysial line *sl* (Figs 35A, 40B, H). Some species also have a supra-ocular ecdysial line, *xl* (Fig. 42G). The additional lines distinguish the final instar without the need to measure head width, but are difficult to see in pale larvae.

Beraeodes minutus (Beraeidae) is very similar to leptocerids, not only in the length and position of the antennae, but also in the long hind legs and slender appearance. The larva (Figs 16A–C), which is radically different from other beraeid larvae, can be distinguished from leptocerids by the mosaic pattern on the pronotum at the final instar and at earlier instars by the numerous setae on the fronto-clypeal apotome (Fig. 35G); (these are pale and are most easily seen with the head in lateral view illuminated from below, or with top light against a dark background). At all instars, leptocerids are characterized by the division of the femora of the second and third legs into short proximal (*fp*) and longer distal (*fd*) sections (Figs 34A–C). A trochanter to femur articulation typical of most other families is exemplified by *Potamophylax latipennis* (Fig. 34D). If the antennal character in couplet 8 of the Key to Families (p. 30) has caused any problems, then the femoral character will help to resolve them. Problems are most likely to have arisen with Molannidae, which have moderately long antennae especially at early instars (Fig. 85E), and superficially resemble leptocerids (Fig. 11H). Molannids are further distinguished from leptocerids by the presence of a process on the tibia of the first leg (Fig. 11E) and the unusual form of the tarsal claw of the third leg (Fig. 11G). Larvae of Odontoceridae, Beraeidae and Sericostomatidae (which, like leptocerids, have the antennae close to the anterior margin of the head capsule) have articulations which could be confused with those of Leptoceridae. In *Odontocerum albicorne* the femur has a dark coloured proximal tip (Fig. 34E) but is all one segment. In Beraeidae and Sericostomatidae the articulation is pale in colour and structures are difficult to distinguish,

TABLE 7. HEAD WIDTHS OF LEPTOCERIDAE
Ranges (and *n*) of head widths (mm) at instars II to V.

Species	Instar			
	II	III	IV	V
Adicella filicornis	—	—	0·34–0·39 (7)	0·49–0·51 (5)
A. reducta	—	0·25 (1)	0·37–0·41 (4)	0·54–0·66 (14)
Athripsodes				
albifrons	—	—	—	0·62–0·89 (73)
A. aterrimus	0·21 (2)	0·29–0·33 (16)	0·44–0·51 (40)	0·63–0·87 (67)
A. bilineatus	—	—	—	0·60–0·73 (23)
A. cinereus	—	0·29–0·40 (19)	0·46–0·57 (34)	0·71–0·88 (93)
A. commutatus	—	—	—	0·63–0·79 (26)
A. albifrons/bilineatus/commutatus	*0·18 (1)	*0·26–0·29 (22)	*0·40–0·50 (51)	—
Ceraclea				
albimacula	†	0·29 (1)	0·45–0·55 (3)	0·82–1·01 (31)
C. annulicornis	0·18 (1)	0·26, 0·27 (2)	0·42–0·50 (17)	0·67–0·87 (81)
C. dissimilis	0·12–0·18 (34)	0·20–0·27 (31)	0·33–0·45 (31)	0·57–0·74 (71)
C. fulva	0·21 (2)	0·32–0·39 (5)	0·55–0·71 (5)	0·84–1·04 (22)
C. nigronervosa	0·21, 0·22 (2)	0·37–0·39 (5)	0·62–0·71 (11)	1·03–1·40 (86)
C. senilis	0·20–0·22 (3)	0·34–0·40 (7)	0·59–0·68 (11)	0·91–1·21 (33)
Erotesis baltica	—	—	0·35–0·40 (4)	0·56 (2)
Leptocerus				
interruptus	—	*0·16–0·18 (4)	0·23–0·24 (10)	0·37–0·44 (14)
L. lusitanicus	—	—	0·23 (1)	0·42–0·48 (20)
L. tineiformis	—	—	0·25–0·27 (5)	0·43–0·55 (31)
Mystacides azurea	—	0·23–0·27 (13)	0·33–0·40 (35)	0·55–0·65 (34)
M. longicornis	0·18–0·19 (6)	0·27–0·30 (6)	0·41–0·49 (16)	0·60–0·77 (16)
M. nigra	—	0·25, 0·29 (2)	0·39–0·43 (11)	0·56–0·69 (14)
Oecetis furva	—	—	0·65, 0·69 (2)	0·83–1·07 (17)
O. lacustris	—	0·28–0·29 (3)	0·41–0·49 (5)	0·71–0·88 (12)
O. notata	—	—	0·43–0·49 (7)	0·77–0·87 (16)
O. ochracea	—	0·39, 0·43 (2)	0·71–0·83 (15)	1·06–1·28 (16)
O. testacea	—	—	0·41–0·46 (5)	0·67–0·76 (38)
Setodes argentipunctellus	0·12–0·13 (10)	0·17–0·21 (18)	0·23–0·29 (17)	0·37–0·41 (28)
S. punctatus	—	—	0·29 (2)	0·39–0·46 (5)
Triaenodes bicolor	0·18–0·22 (11)	0·28–0·34 (25)	0·39–0·48 (39)	0·59–0·88 (61)
Ylodes conspersus	*0·18, 0·21 (2)	*0·27–0·32 (8)	0·39–0·49 (14)	0·71–0·82 (22)
Y. reuteri	—	—	—	0·67–0·87 (6)
Y. simulans	—	—	*0·35–0·41 (9)	0·51–0·69 (43)

*Not keyed to species at this instar.
†Examined at this instar but not measured.

but a line marking off the proximal end of the femur can be seen easily in *Beraeodes minutus* (Fig. 34F) and with difficulty in the other species (Figs 34G, H). However, unlike leptocerids, there does not appear to be a separate sclerite in these families.

The third legs are much longer than the others and in some genera the tibia (and the tarsus in *Mystacides*) has a central constriction and pale band (*c*, Fig 34C). This feature, which is also present in Molannidae, allows slight flexion of the segment. A few species of leptocerids have setal fringes on the third legs (Figs 35E, F) which enable the larva to swim well with its case by rapidly rowing the legs. No other cased caddis can swim so proficiently. Also unusual among cased caddis are the long, single-bladed jaws of *Oecetis*, used to capture worms and chironomid larvae which are swallowed whole.

The leptocerid pupal case has a single posterior opening through which the moulted larval sclerites are vigorously ejected. Pupal cases are therefore much less useful for identification than those of other families, where the sclerites are retained by a grille or restricted opening. The ejection of the sclerites may be done to prevent damage to the antennae, which are coiled round the posterior end of the pupa.

Before using the key it is important to be familiar with the following features which are used in a number of couplets, sometimes without specific illustration.

Setal arrangement on the mesoventer and metaventer and 1st abdominal venter   (Figs 35C, D). Setal counts are usually quoted as 'on each side' of the mid-line. Sometimes, however, the two setal groups merge to give a continuous band and in such cases total numbers are quoted. It is always important to exclude from counts the seta *ps*, associated with each pleurite, and the seta *ls*, associated with each lateral sclerite on the 1st abdominal segment.

Protrochantin.   This is fairly large in the leptocerids; its location is shown as *pt* in Fig. 35B.

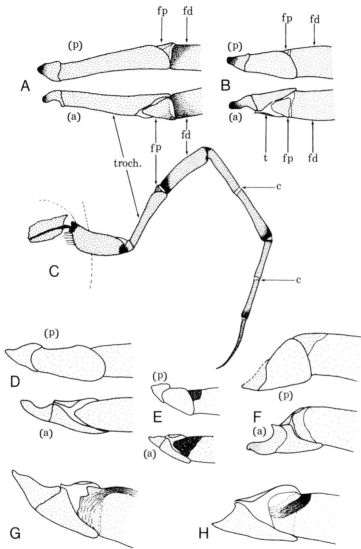

Fig. 34. **A, B**: trochanter and proximal end of femur, anterior (a) and posterior (p) views: A, 3rd leg of *Mystacides longicornis*; B, 2nd leg of *Ceraclea annulicornis*. **C**: metapleurite and 3rd leg, posterior view, of *M. longicornis*. **D–F**: trochanter and proximal end of femur of 3rd leg, anterior (a) and posterior (p) views: D, *Potamophylax latipennis*; E, *Odontocerum albicorne*; F, *Beraeodes minutus*. **G, H**: trochanter and proximal end of femur, anterior view, of *Sericostoma personatum*: G, 2nd leg; H, 3rd leg.

Key to larvae

(i) Fronto-clypeal apotome with numerous setae (Fig. 35G)—
Beraeodes minutus (L.)
(Family BERAEIDAE, p. 42)

Pronotum with a black mosaic pattern most obvious at instar V (Fig. 35H).

— Fronto-clypeal apotome with only 10 setae—
Family LEPTOCERIDAE, **1**

Pronotum never with a mosaic pattern though it may have colour patches.

1   Tarsal claw *c* of 2nd leg hook-shaped (Fig. 36A)—
Genus LEPTOCERUS, **2**

(*Leptocerus* species are not separable at instars II and III: head width less than 0·20 mm).

3rd leg always with long anterior and posterior setal fringes (arranged as in Figs 35E, F) which enable the larva to swim.

— Tarsal claw *c* of 2nd leg curved but never hook-shaped (Fig. 38A)—
4

In a few species, the 3rd leg has long setal fringes (Figs 35E, F) which enable the larva to swim.

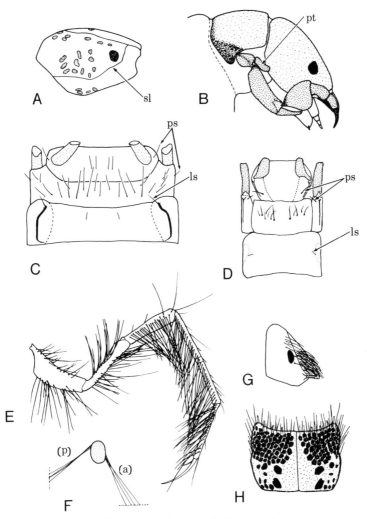

Fig. 35. **A**: head capsule, lateral view, of *Athripsodes cinereus*. **B**: head and prothorax, lateral view, of *Mystacides longicornis*. **C, D**: mesothorax, metathorax and 1st abdominal segment, ventral view: C, *Ceraclea fulva*; D, *Leptocerus tineiformis*. **E, F**: 3rd leg of *Triaenodes bicolor*: E, posterior view; F, diagrammatic transverse section of tibia. **G, H**: *Beraeodes minutus* (Beraeidae): G, head capsule, lateral view, instar IV; H, pronotum, instar V.

2 Distal part of anal proleg with 5 long setae AND a number of small
   setae *ps* (Fig. 36B); (avoid confusion with setae on the basal lobes, *ls*
   in Figs 36B, C). Metadorsum with 1 long and 1 or more short anterior-
   lateral setae. Case almost straight, of translucent secreted material
   (Fig. 36F)—   **Leptocerus tineiformis** Curtis
                                                        Instars IV and V

> Lakes, large weedy ponds and occasionally canals. Mainly midland
> and southern England; absent from Scotland and Ireland.

— Distal part of anal proleg with 5 long setae only (Fig. 36C). Metadorsum with only 1 anterior-lateral seta *al* (Fig. 36D). Case curved, of
   secreted material with numerous embedded sand grains, at least in
   the posterior half (Fig. 36G)—   **3**

3 Mesonotum central area with 2 or 3 setae *cs* (Fig. 36D). Metaventer
   with several setae on each side (as in Fig. 35D). Protrochantin central
   region pale (Fig. 36H) and similar in colour to the central area of the
   face of the 1st leg coxa—   **Leptocerus interruptus** (Fabricius)
                                                        Instars IV and V

> Among vegetation, including tree roots, in slow-flowing regions of
> rivers. Records from Devon, Somerset, Gwent, Hereford & Wor-
> cester.

— Mesonotum central area with 7–12 setae *cs* (Fig. 36E). Metaventer
   with only 1 seta on each side. Protrochantin central region dark (Fig.
   36I), contrasting with the central area of the face of the 1st leg coxa—
                                    Leptocerus lusitanicus (McLachlan)
                                                        Instars IV and V

> In slow-flowing water among submerged *Salix* roots. Only recorded
> from the River Thames and its tributary, the Thame, on the Oxford-
> shire/Berkshire border.

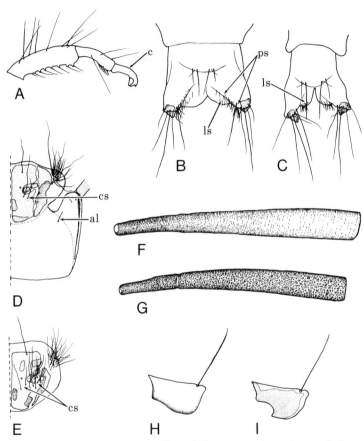

Fig. 36.   **A**: tibia and tarsus of 2nd leg, posterior view, of *Leptocerus tineiformis*.   **B, C**: 9th abdominal segment, dorsal view: B, *L. tineiformis*; C, *L. interruptus*.   **D**: mesodorsum and metadorsum, right half, of *L. interruptus*.   **E**: mesodorsum, right half, of *L. lusitanicus*.   **F, G**: case: F, *L. tineiformis*; G, *L. lusitanicus*.   **H, I**: protrochantin: H, *L. interruptus*; I, *L. lusitanicus*.

4(1) Mandibles about 3 times as long as their width at the base (Figs 37B, D) and with only 1 cutting edge (Fig. 37B). Labrum with numerous setae on the dorsal surface (Fig. 37C)—   Genus OECETIS, 5

> (*Oecetis* species are not separable at instar II: head width less than 0·25 mm).

—   Mandibles at most twice as long as their width at the base and with 2 cutting edges, one dorsal and one ventral (Fig. 37A). Labrum with few setae on the dorsal surface (Figs 41A, B)—   **9**

5   Mesoventer with 1–4 setae on each side; metaventer with a total of 17–60 setae. Tarsal claw of 2nd and 3rd legs with a rudimentary basal seta (arrow, Fig. 37E)—   **6**

—   Mesoventer without setae; metaventer with only 1–6 setae. Tarsal claw of 2nd and 3rd legs with a prominent basal seta (arrow, Fig. 37F)—   **7**

6   Protrochantin with several long dark setae (Fig. 37G). 9th abdominal dorsum with 12 setae (Fig. 37J)—   **Oecetis lacustris** (Pictet)
                                                                          Instars III to V

> Case curved and tapering, composed of sand grains.

> Lakes, large ponds, canals and slow-flowing rivers; muddy sand substrata and among tree roots. Widespread.

—   Protrochantin with only 1 long dark seta (Fig. 37H). 9th abdominal dorsum with more than 12 setae (up to 40 at instar V, Fig. 37K)—
                                                    Oecetis ochracea (Curtis)
                                                                          Instars III to V

> Case curved, smooth, composed of sand grains, other small particles or a mixture of the two; very fragile compared with other caddis cases.

> Lakes, large ponds and canals; muddy and sandy substrata, often under several metres of water. Early colonizer of new reservoirs and lakes. Widespread and common.

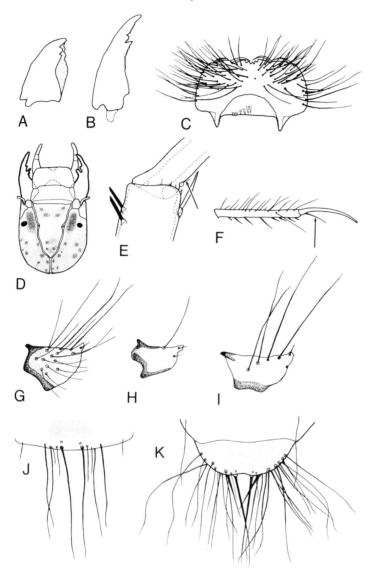

Fig. 37. **A**: right mandible, ventral view, of *Ceraclea fulva*. **B**: left mandible, dorsal view, of *Oecetis furva*. **C**: labrum, dorsal view of *O. ochracea*. **D**: head of *O. ochracea*. **E, F**: 3rd leg, posterior view: E, articular region of tarsus and claw of *O. ochracea*; F, tarsus and claw of *O. furva*. **G–I**: protrochantin: G, *O. lacustris*; H, *O. ochracea*; I, *O. notata*. **J, K**: part of 9th abdominal dorsum: J, *O. lacustris*; K, *O. ochracea*.

7(5) Note: Separation has not been tested at instar III (head width less than 0·40 mm).

Head and thoracic dorsal sclerites of a very pale straw colour, entirely lacking coloured patches or colour associated with muscle attachment spots. Protrochantin with more than 1 long dark seta (4 present at instar V, Fig. 37I)— **Oecetis notata** (Rambur)

Instars IV and V

> 3rd legs with 2 long setal fringes (resembling Figs 35E, F) which enable the larva to swim; this it does only reluctantly. Case dorso-ventrally flattened, composed of moss leaves.

> In moderately flowing regions of large rivers; moss-covered stones, tree roots. Recent records from Rivers Tamar, Teifi, Towy and lower Wye and from Ireland.

— Head and thoracic dorsal sclerites with coloured patches and colour associated with muscle attachment spots (Fig. 38B). Protrochantin with only 1 long dark seta (as in Fig. 37H)— 8

8 Note: Separation has not been tested at instar III (head width less than 0·40 mm).

3rd leg with 2 long setal fringes, most easily seen on the tibia (resembling Figs 35E, F). Posterior dorsal margin of head with 3 pale muscle attachment spots on each side of the coronal suture (arrows, Fig. 38D). Larval case robust, with a flattened ventral face, and made of pieces of plant material, particularly roots (Figs 38F, G). 8th abdominal dorsum with all setae much shorter than those of the 9th abdominal dorsum— **Oecetis testacea** (Curtis)

Instars IV and V

> Larva may swim if disturbed.

> Lake shores, rivers and canals; most numerous among stones under plants. Widespread and locally common but apparently absent from eastern England.

— 3rd leg without long setal fringes (Fig. 38A). Posterior dorsal margin of head with 2 pale muscle attachment spots on each side of the coronal suture (arrows, Fig. 38C). Larval case fragile, not flattened, made from plant fragments (Fig. 38E). 8th abdominal dorsum with 1 long seta on each side which is about the size of the longer setae of the 9th abdominal dorsum— **Oecetis furva** (Rambur)

Instars IV and V

> Lakes and large ponds; among marginal plants. Widespread but local.

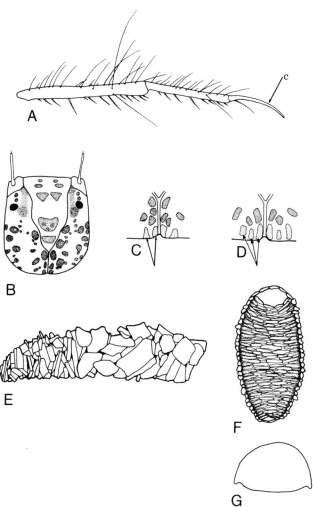

Fig. 38. **A**: tibia and tarsus of 3rd leg, posterior view, of *Oecetis furva*. **B**: head capsule of *O. furva*. **C, D**: posterior region of head adjacent to coronal suture: C, *O. furva*; D, *O. testacea*. **E**: case of *O. furva*. **F, G**: case of *O. testacea*: F, ventral view; G, outline of transverse section.

9(4) Mesonotum with posterior-lateral projections which are usually very dark in colour (arrows, Fig. 39A); (these may be hidden in the intersegmental fold). At least at instar V, most gills consist of several filaments—   **10**

— Mesonotum without posterior-lateral projections. If gills are present each consists of a single unbranched filament—
Genera ADICELLA, EROTESIS, MYSTACIDES, SETODES, TRIAENODES, YLODES, **28**

10 Ventral apotome (arrow, Fig 39B) is triangular; even in small larvae the triangle is taller than its width at base (Fig. 39C). Gills never present on abdominal segments 4–8. Case without an overhanging dorsal lip (Figs 39F, G); composed of sand grains—
Genus ATHRIPSODES, **11**

— Ventral apotome (arrow, Fig. 39D) is quadrangular or polygonal; small larvae may have a triangular apotome but, if so, it is shorter than its width at base and has a rounded apex (Fig. 39E). Gills may be present on abdominal segments 4–8. Case with an overhanging dorsal lip (Figs 39H, I); composed of sand grains, secretion or a mixture of the two—   Genus CERACLEA, **17**

11 Anterior face of trochanter and proximal part of distal section of femur of 3rd leg with many short dagger-shaped orange or straw-coloured setae (*ds* in Figs 39J, K; avoid confusion with spinule combs *sc*)—   **Athripsodes aterrimus** (Stephens)

Ventral side of head, including apotome, generally pale in colour. Dark muscle attachment spots apparent in dorsal, lateral and ventral views of the head (Figs 39B, 40A) and on the pronotum and mesonotum (Fig. 39A). 9th abdominal dorsal sclerite and lateral sclerite of the anal proleg dark brown.

Ponds, lakes and slow-flowing waters, also faster flowing water of lake outlets and below weirs; usually among plants and on muddy sand. Widespread and common.

— Anterior face of trochanter and femur of 3rd leg without any short dagger-shaped setae; setae present on these parts have long tapering tips, and many are brown in colour—   **12**

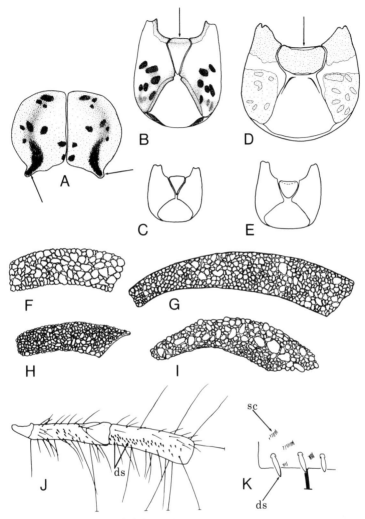

Fig. 39. **A**: mesonotum of *Athripsodes aterrimus*. **B–E**: head capsule, ventral view: B, *A. aterrimus*; C, *A.* ?*albifrons*, instar II; D, *Ceraclea senilis*; E, *C. senilis*, instar II. **F–I**: case: F, *A.* ?*albifrons*, instar II; G, *A. albifrons*; H, *C. dissimilis*, instar II; I, *C. annulicornis*. **J**: trochanter and femur of 3rd leg, anterior view, of *A. aterrimus*. **K**: proximo-ventral region of distal section of femur of 3rd leg, anterior view, of *A. aterrimus*, instar II.

12   Ventral edge of tibia of 1st leg with 1 or 2 setae in addition to the
      single seta *ts* at the distal end (Figs 40D, E; beware confusion with
      large spines)—   **Athripsodes cinereus** (Curtis)
                                                        Instars IV and V

      Ventral apotome and adjacent parts of the head very dark brown or
      black (Fig. 40C). Lateral part of the head with distinct dark muscle
      attachment spots which are almost equivalent in intensity to those
      on the fronto-clypeal apotome and alongside the frontoclypeal suture
      (Figs 35A, 40B); (these spots are not visible in a melanic form fairly
      common in Mochrum Loch, Wigtownshire).

      Rivers, streams, lakes and canals; stony and sandy substrata. Wide-
      spread and common.

—   Ventral edge of tibia of 1st leg with only a single seta *ts*, which is at
      the distal end (Fig. 40F)—   **13**

13   Subocular ecdysial line *sl* (Figs 35A, 40B) makes a pale gap in the
      darkly coloured posterior ridge of the head capsule (Fig. 40H)—**14**

—   No subocular ecdysial line or pale gap in the darkly coloured posterior
      ridge of the head capsule; (ridge may be narrowed at a similar position,
      n in Fig. 40G)—   **16**

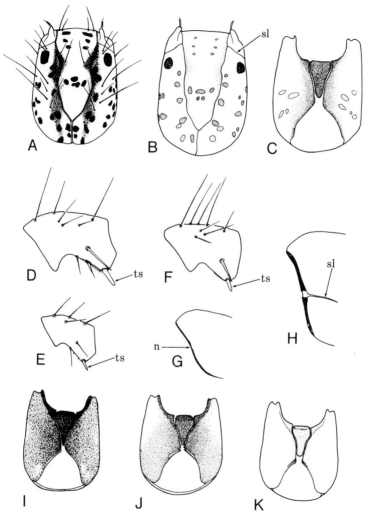

Fig. 40. **A**: head capsule of *Athripsodes aterrimus*. **B, C**: head capsule of *A. cinereus*: B, dorsal view; C, ventral view. **D–F**: tibia of 1st leg, anterior view: D, *A. cinereus*; E, *A. cinereus*, instar IV; F, *A. bilineatus*. **G, H**: posterior part of head capsule, lateral view, of *A. bilineatus*: G, instar IV; H, instar V. **I–K**: head capsule, ventral view: I, *A. bilineatus*; J, *A. albifrons*; K, *A. commutatus*.

14 The dark purse-shaped mark *m* in the middle of the anterior part of the labrum usually lies clear of the median pit *p* (Figs 41A, C); if the two abut, the posterior margin of the mark is not inflexed at that point (Fig. 41D); (this feature is best seen on a detached labrum using transmitted light)—   **Athripsodes bilineatus** (L.)
                                                               Instar V

> Stony substratum; large streams and rivers throughout Britain, also small streams in south-east England and lake shores in Scotland. Most frequent in northern and western Britain, rare in Ireland.

> NOTE: A small proportion (less than 5%) of *A. albifrons* and *A. commutatus* appear here. They will not comply with at least one of the following characters. Metadorsum with the outer setae of the median quartet *q* over half the length of the inner pair (usually at least three-quarters, as shown in Fig. 41L). Muscle attachment spots *fp* on the posterior part of the frontoclypeal apotome are equivalent in intensity to those *lp* on the parietals bordering the fronto-clypeal suture (Fig. 41N); the lateral spots *lp* may merge with a band of colour. Ventral apotome with a pointed apex (Fig. 40I).

— The purse-shaped mark *m* in the middle of the anterior part of the labrum has its posterior margin deeply invaginated around the median pit *p* (Fig. 41B); occasionally the margin apparently overlaps the pits (Figs 41E–J) or the two abut, in which case the margin is inflexed at that point (Fig. 41K)—   **15**

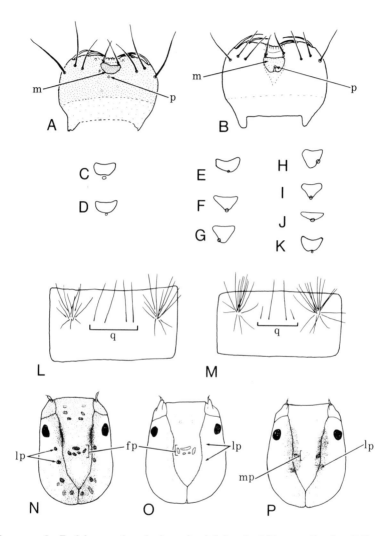

Fig. 41. **A, B**: labrum, dorsal view: A, *Athripsodes bilineatus*; B, *A. albifrons*. **C–K**: various arrangements of the purse-shaped mark and median pit of the labrum: C, D, *A. bilineatus*; E–G, *A. commutatus*; H–K, *A. albifrons*. **L, M**: metadorsum: L, *A. bilineatus*; M, *A. albifrons*. **N–P**: head capsule: N, *A. bilineatus*; O, *A. commutatus*; P, *A. albifrons*.

15   Metadorsum with the outer setae of the median quartet q less than
     half the length of the inner pair (usually one-third, as shown in Fig.
     41M). Median muscle attachment spots mp on the posterior part of
     the fronto-clypeal apotome are definitely paler than those lp on the
     parietals bordering the fronto-clypeal suture (Fig. 41P); the lateral
     spots lp may merge with a band of colour. Ventral apotome with
     pointed apex (Fig. 40J)—   **Athripsodes albifrons** (L.)
                                                              Instar V

          A small proportion of larvae will conform to only two of the three
          characters given above.

          Stony substratum. Common in rivers everywhere except highland
          Scotland where it is very local; also on lake shores in Ireland.

—   Metadorsum with the outer setae of the median quartet q over half
     the length of the inner pair (usually two-thirds). Muscle attachment
     spots fp on the posterior part of the fronto-clypeal apotome are
     definitely darker than those lp on the parietals bordering the fronto-
     clypeal suture (Fig. 41O); (in very pale individuals the lateral spots
     lp are absent); the band of colour running adjacent to the fronto-
     clypeal suture, if apparent, is extremely pale. Ventral apotome with
     rounded apex (Fig. 40K)—   **Athripsodes commutatus** (Rostock)
                                                              Instar V

          A small proportion of larvae will conform to only two of the three
          characters given above.

          Stony substratum; rivers. Common in Scotland and Ireland; very
          local in northern England, southern Wales and south-west England;
          old isolated records of adults from elsewhere.

16(13) Note: Separation has not been tested at instar II (head width less than 0·25 mm).

Distinct muscle attachment spots apparent on the mesonotum, pronotum and lateral parts of the head capsule. No coloured bands on the parietals adjacent to the fronto-clypeal suture—

Athripsodes cinereus (Curtis)
Instar III

See couplet 12 for habitat.

— Muscle attachment spots not visible on the mesonotum; spots on the pronotum and lateral parts of the head capsule, if present, are irregular and very pale. There may be a brown band on the parietals adjacent to the fronto-clypeal suture (as in Fig. 41P)—

Athripsodes albifrons (L.)
Athripsodes bilineatus (L.)
Athripsodes commutatus (Rostock)
Instars III and IV

17(10) 3rd leg with 2 long setal fringes (Fig. 42A, arranged as in Fig. 42B); larva may swim. Very small larva, head width around 0·2 mm and case length less than 2·5 mm—

Genus CERACLEA, Instar II, **23**

— 3rd leg without 2 long setal fringes (Figs 42C, D); larva does not swim. Larger larva—　　Genus CERACLEA, Instars III to V, **18**

18　Mesoventer with setae (Fig. 35C)—　　　　　　　　　　　　**19**

— Mesoventer without setae—　　　　　　　　　　　　　　**20**

19　Mesoventer with 1 seta on each side. Pronotum generally brown, without a very dark band along the anterior edge (Fig. 42E). Head brown with a pattern of dark muscle attachment spots (Fig. 42G). Protrochantin covered with prominent spinules (Figs 43A, B) and with distal end *d* prolonged at instars IV and V (Fig. 43A; head width more than 0·50 mm). Anal proleg claw with 1 accessory hook (arrow, Figs 44C, D)—　　　　　　　　　**Ceraclea senilis** (Burmeister)

Instars III to V

> Case composed of translucent flexible secreted material and sponge spicules; living pieces of sponge sometimes attached to the outside of the case.

> Still or slow-flowing water; in sponges. Ireland, midland and southern England, Dumfries & Galloway; local.

— Mesoventer with 2 or more setae on each side (Fig. 35C). Pronotum pale with a distinctive very dark band along the anterior edge (Fig. 42F). Head pale, without a distinct colour pattern (Fig. 42H). Protrochantin with neither prominent spinules nor a prolonged distal end (as in Fig. 43C). Anal proleg claw with 2 accessory hooks (as in Figs 44A, B)—　　　　　　　　　　**Ceraclea fulva** (Rambur)

Instars III to V

> Case composed of translucent, flexible secreted material and sponge spicules, frequently with living pieces of sponge attached to the outside (Fig. 44I).

> Large ponds and lakes; in sponges. Widespread; common except in south-east England.

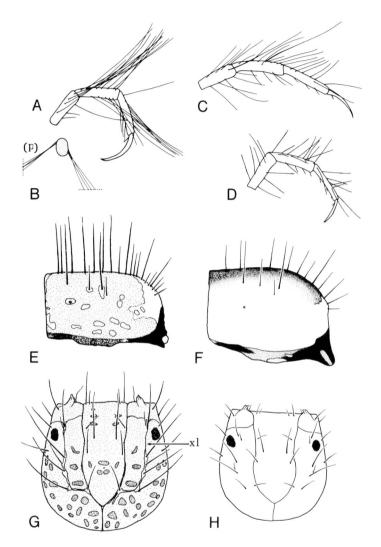

Fig. 42.   **A, C, D**: femur, tibia and tarsus of 3rd leg, posterior view, of *Ceraclea
dissimilis*: A, instar II; C, instar III; D, instar V.   **B**: diagrammatic
transverse section of tibia of 3rd leg of *C. dissimilis*, instar II.   **E, F**:
pronotum, right half: E, *C. senilis*; F, *C. fulva*.   **G, H**: head capsule:
G, *C. senilis*; H, *C. fulva*.

20(18) Metaventer with 2 or more setae on each side—   21

— Metaventer with only 1 seta on each side—   22

21   Case composed of closely abutted sand grains (Fig. 43D), occasionally
     with roots incorporated at the anterior end. 9th abdominal dorsum
     with two groups of 3 setae (arrows, Fig. 43F), all smaller than the
     innermost setae *ps* of the anal proleg lateral sclerites (Fig. 43F).
     Rarely found in sponges—   **Ceraclea dissimilis** (Stephens)
                                                          Instars III to V

> Head pale in colour at all instars. Anal proleg claw with 2 accessory
> hooks (as in Figs 44A, B).
>
> Rivers, large streams and stony lake shores; on and under big stones,
> also on submerged tree roots but only in slow-flowing water. Wide-
> spread and common.

—   Case composed of tough flexible secreted material with bands of
     embedded sand grains (Fig. 43E). 9th abdominal dorsum with two
     groups of 4 setae (arrows, Fig. 43G) each having at least one seta as
     long as the innermost setae *ps* of the anal proleg lateral sclerites (Fig.
     43G). Usually associated with sponges—
                                            Ceraclea nigronervosa (Retzius)
                                                          Instars III to V

> Instar V head with a distinctive pattern of dark brown patches (Fig.
> 43H); younger larvae have pale heads (Fig. 43I). Anal proleg claw
> with 1 or 2 accessory hooks.
>
> Streams, rivers and lakes; stony substratum. Widespread and com-
> mon. Overwinters as fully grown larva in pupal case.

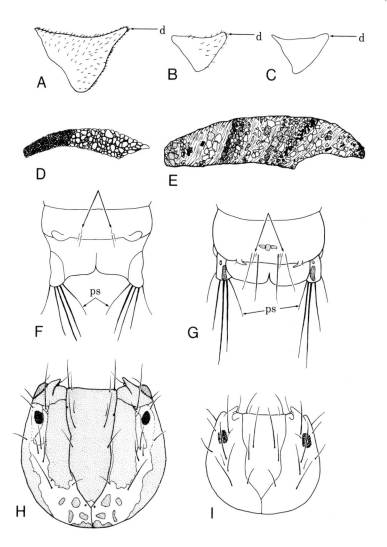

Fig. 43. **A–C**: protrochantin: A, *Ceraclea senilis*; B, *C. senilis*, instar III; C, *C. nigronervosa*. **D, E**: case: D, *C. dissimilis*, instar III; E, *C. nigronervosa*. **F, G**: 9th abdominal segment, dorsal view: F, *C. dissimilis*; G, *C. nigronervosa*. **H, I**: head capsule of *C. nigronervosa*: H, instar V; I, instar IV.

22(20) Case EITHER composed entirely of translucent, flexible secreted
material without embedded sand grains (but sometimes with added
pieces of sponge, as in Fig. 44I) OR (at instar III only) with a posterior
end of closely abutted sand grains and an anterior end of secretion
(Fig. 44H). Metadorsum with up to 3 setae in each anterior-lateral
group *al*, at least 1 of which is longer than the median setae *m* (Fig.
44E). Anal proleg claw with 2 accessory hooks (arrows, Figs 44A,
B). In sponges—   **Ceraclea albimacula** (Rambur)
                                                  Instars III to V

> Head pale with faint muscle attachment spots at all instars. Tibia of
> 2nd leg without short setae on the ventral edge.

> Rivers, large streams and canals. Widespread. Overwinters at instar
> II (but not necessarily in sponges).

—   Case always composed entirely of closely abutted sand grains (Fig.
39I). Metadorsum with more than 3 setae in each anterior-lateral
group *al* (6–12 at instar V, Fig. 44G), the longest of which are
comparable with the median setae *m* (Fig. 44G). Anal proleg claw
with 1 accessory hook (as in Figs 44C, D). Not found in sponges—
                                       Ceraclea annulicornis (Stephens)
                                                  Instars III to V

> Head reddish-orange at instar V, pale at earlier instars. Tibia of 2nd
> leg with 1–3 short setae on the ventral edge (arrows, Fig. 44F, instars
> IV and V only).

> Rivers, also occasionally on lake shores; associated with large stones.
> Widespread and common in Britain, rarer in Ireland. Overwinters at
> instar V.

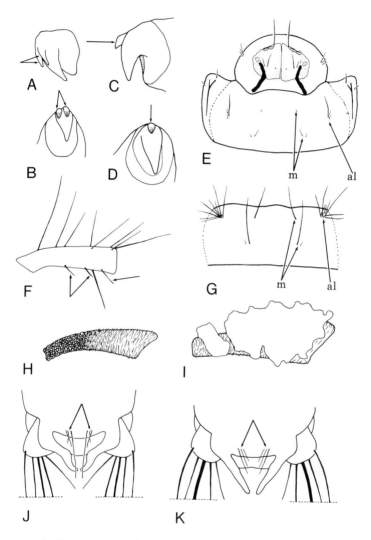

Fig. 44. **A–D**: anal proleg claw and accessory hook(s): A, B, *Ceraclea albimacula*; C, D, *C. senilis*. **E**: mesothorax and metathorax, dorsal view, of *C. albimacula*. **F**: tibia of 2nd leg, anterior view, of *C. annulicornis*. **G**: metadorsum of *C. annulicornis*. **H, I**: case: H, *C. albimacula*, instar III; I, *C. fulva*. **J, K**: 9th abdominal segment, dorsal view: J, *C. nigronervosa*, instar II; K, *C. dissimilis*, instar II.

23(17) Mesoventer with setae. Case composed principally of translucent flexible secreted material; sand grains not incorporated—   **24**

—   Mesoventer without setae. Case composed, at least in part, of sand grains—   **25**

24   Mesoventer with 2 setae on each side—   **Ceraclea fulva** (Rambur)
                                                            Instar II
            See couplet 19 for habitat.

—   Mesoventer with 1 seta on each side—
                                            Ceraclea senilis (Burmeister)
                                                            Instar II
            See couplet 19 for habitat.

25(23) Metaventer with 2 setae on each side—   **26**

—   Metaventer with 1 seta on each side—   **27**

26   9th abdominal dorsum with 1 seta in each group which is much
      thicker and longer than the others (arrows, Fig. 44J). Found from
      June to early August—   **Ceraclea nigronervosa** (Retzius)
                                                              Instar II

            See couplet 21 for habitat.

—   9th abdominal dorsum with all setae in each group more or less alike
      (arrows, Fig. 44K). Found from August to April—
                                        Ceraclea dissimilis (Stephens)
                                                              Instar II

            See couplet 21 for habitat.

27(25) Found from August to May—

                                        Ceraclea albimacula (Rambur)
                                                              Instar II

            See couplet 22 for habitat.

—   Found from July to September— **Ceraclea annulicornis** (Stephens)
                                                              Instar II

            See couplet 22 for habitat.

28(9) EITHER: anal region surrounded by tooth-edged plates *tp* (Figs 45C, E); OR: anal prolegs with two rows of strong posteriorly directed spines *pp* (Figs 45B, D). Case of sand grains, curved but not conspicuously tapering (Fig. 45G)—   Genus SETODES, **29**

—   Anal region with neither tooth-edged plates nor rows of strong posteriorly directed spines on the prolegs; (there may be spinules *p* and large soft spines *sp* around the anal slit, as in Fig. 45A)—   **30**

29   Note: Setal counts are not known for instars II and III (head width less than 0·23 mm).
Anal proleg with two rows of strong posteriorly directed spines *pp* (Figs 45B, D). 1st abdominal segment with only 1 or 2 dorso-lateral setae *dl* (Fig. 45F) and 1 ventral seta on each side. Metadorsum central area with only 4 setae *cs* (Fig. 45F). Metaventer with up to 12 setae. Sclerites greyish-brown—
Setodes argentipunctellus (McLachlan)

> Lake shores; stony substratum. Windermere and Coniston Water (English Lake District), Mochrum Loch (Dumfries & Galloway), Lower and Middle Lakes (Killarney, Ireland); extremely local, being absent from neighbouring lakes; often abundant where found.

—   Anal region surrounded by tooth-edged plates *tp* (Figs 45C, E). 1st abdominal segment with more than 2 dorso-lateral setae and more than 1 ventral seta on each side. Metadorsum central area with many more than 4 setae (about 20). Metaventer with many more than 12 setae (about 60). Sclerites straw-coloured—
Setodes punctatus (Fabricius)

> Fast-flowing regions of large rivers; sandy substratum. Rivers Severn and Wye (England).

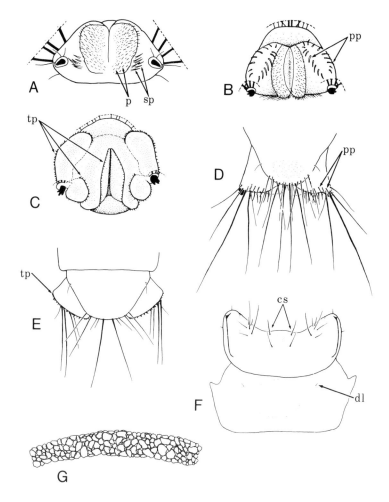

Fig. 45.   **A–C**: 9th abdominal segment, posterior view: A, *Mystacides longicornis*; B, *Setodes argentipunctellus*; C, *S. punctatus*. **D, E**: 9th abdominal segment, dorsal view: D, *S. argentipunctellus*; E, *S. punctatus*. **F**: metathorax and 1st abdominal segment, dorsal view, of *S. argentipunctellus*. **G**: case of *S. argentipunctellus*.

30(28) 1st abdominal lateral sclerite (*f* in Fig. 46A) with a posterior projection bearing a conspicuous dark bar *b* (Figs 46B, D); (in larvae with a head width of less than 0·2 mm, the bar is rather thin and could be overlooked, Fig. 46C)— **31**

— 1st abdominal lateral sclerite without a dark bar on its posterior projection (Fig. 46E); (sclerite may range from pale straw to grey in colour)— **36**

31 Tibia and tarsus of 3rd leg each with a median constriction *c* (Fig. 34C), usually marked by a pale transverse band; (these features are difficult to detect in very small larvae). Dark bar of posterior projection of 1st abdominal lateral sclerite is thin and curved (Figs 46B, C). Head, pronotum and mesonotum with black spots on a yellowish or brownish background. Case straight or slightly curved, of sand grains usually with added plant fragments (Figs 46H, I)—
Genus MYSTACIDES, **32**

— Neither tibia nor tarsus of 3rd leg with a median constriction or pale transverse band. Dark bar of posterior projection of 1st abdominal lateral sclerite is broad and straight (Fig. 46D). Head with reddish-orange colouration, pronotum and mesonotum very pale brown with slightly darker spots. Case EITHER strongly curved, composed of sand grains coated with secretion (Fig. 46F) OR straight, composed of pieces of plant material, usually roots, arranged in a spiral (Fig. 46G)—
Genus ADICELLA, **35**

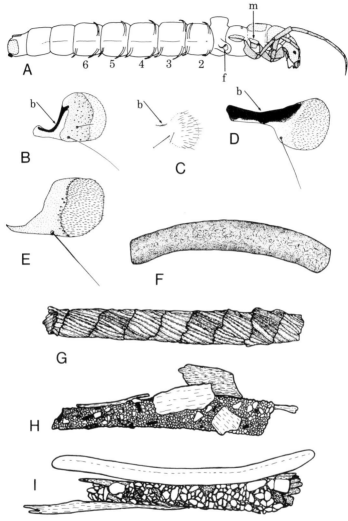

Fig. 46. **A**: larva of *Mystacides longicornis*, lateral view. **B–E**: 1st abdominal lateral sclerite: B, *M. longicornis*; C, *M. longicornis*, instar II; D, *Adicella reducta*; E, *Triaenodes bicolor*. **F–I**: case: F, *A. filicornis*; G, *A. reducta*; H, *M. longicornis*; I, *M. azurea*.

32 Gills present on 6th abdominal segment (Fig. 46A)—
                                  Mystacides longicornis (L.)
                                  Instar V (most key out here)

  Large ponds, lakes, canals and very slowly flowing large rivers; muddy sand substrata and among vegetation. Widespread and common.

— Gills absent from 6th abdominal segment—   **33**

33 Posterior half of fronto-clypeal apotome with a distinctively shaped mark (Fig. 47A). Anal proleg claw with 2 obvious accessory hooks (arrows, Figs 47D, E); sometimes a minute hook *m* is present above the claw (Fig. 47E). Ventral part of anterior faces of trochanters and femora of 2nd and 3rd legs with long dagger-like spinules at instar V (head width more than 0·50 mm) and numerous spinule combs *sc* and short dagger-like spinules *dp* at earlier instars (Fig. 47F); (a magnification of ×200 may be required)—   **34**

— Posterior half of fronto-clypeal apotome with a pattern of spots, not a distinctively shaped mark (Fig. 47B). Anal proleg claw with 3 obvious accessory hooks (arrows, Fig. 47C), one of which is directly above the claw. Ventral part of anterior faces of trochanters and femora of 2nd and 3rd legs without prominent dagger-like spinules or large spinule combs; (a few small spinule combs may be present)—
                                  Mystacides azurea (L.)

  In most specimens, gills are absent from all abdominal segments, but a few larvae have been found which agree with all of the characters given above except that they possess gills. They seem to be very rare and none has yet been reared to the adult.

  Lakes, canals and still or slow-flowing regions of rivers and large streams; stony substratum or tree roots and other vegetation. Widespread and common.

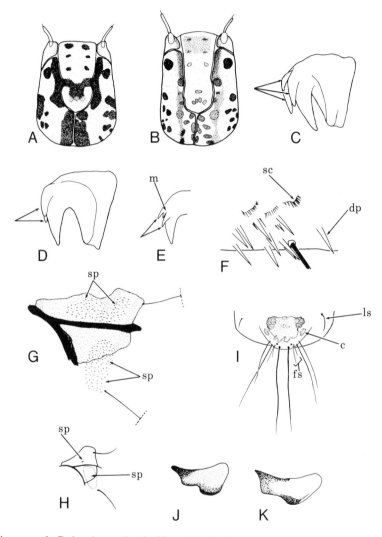

Fig. 47. **A, B**: head capsule: A, *Mystacides longicornis*; B, *M. azurea*. **C–E**: anal proleg claw and accessory hooks: C, *M. azurea*; D, *M. longicornis*; E, *M. nigra*. **F**: mid-ventral region of femur of 3rd leg, anterior view, of *M. longicornis*, instar IV. **G, H**: mesopleurite of *M. longicornis*: G, instar V; H, instar II. **I**: 9th abdominal dorsum of *M. longicornis*. **J, K**: protrochantin: J, *M. longicornis*; K, *M. nigra*.

34 Mesopleurite (*m*, Fig. 46A) with a patch *sp* of spinule combs to each
side of the central bar (Fig. 47G; these spinule combs resemble those
shown (enlarged) as *sc* in Fig. 47F); at instars II and III (head width
less than 0·35 mm) dorsal patch may be represented by only 1 or 2
short spinule combs (as in Fig. 47H); (a magnification of at least ×200
should be used)—   **Mystacides longicornis** (L.)

> Femur of 3rd leg with large dagger-like spinules on ventral part of
> anterior face at instar V, dagger-like spinules and spinule combs at
> earlier instars. Except in dark larvae (characterized by grey-brown
> to black parietals), 9th abdominal segment at instar V with lateral
> colour patches *c* on the dorsal sclerite (Fig. 47I) and posterior-lateral
> setae *ls* which are dark and similar in colour to the fine dorsal sclerite
> setae *fs* (Fig. 47I); at instars IV and V, protrochantin central area
> grey-brown (Fig. 47J) and darker than central area of 1st leg coxa.
>
> See couplet 32 for habitat.

— Mesopleurite with a patch of spinule combs only to the ventral side
of the central bar—   **Mystacides nigra** (L.)

> Femur of 3rd leg with dagger-like spinules and spinule combs on
> ventral part of anterior face at instar V (as in Fig. 47F), but only
> spinule combs at other instars. 9th abdominal segment without lateral
> colour patches *c* on the dorsal sclerite and with posterior-lateral setae
> *ls* which are paler than the fine dorsal sclerite setae *fs* (see Fig.
> 47I). Except in dark larvae (characterized by grey-brown to black
> parietals), protrochantin central area straw-coloured (Fig. 47K) and
> similar in colour to central area of 1st leg coxa.
>
> Lakes, canals and still or slow-flowing regions of rivers and large
> streams; stony substratum or tree roots and other vegetation.
> Throughout England and Wales; also in central Scotland. Usually
> found in small numbers with one or both of the other *Mystacides*
> species.

35(31) Note: Separation has not been tested at instars II and III (head width less than 0·30 mm).

Case straight, composed of pieces of plant material, usually roots, arranged in a spiral (Fig. 46G). 9th abdominal dorsum with 12 setae (Fig. 48A). Excluding anterior-lateral setal groups *al*, mesodorsum with up to 10 setae (usually 8) and metadorsum with only 4 setae (Fig. 48C)—   **Adicella reducta** (McLachlan)

> Head pale with reddish-orange bands and spots (Fig. 48D) at instar V (ventral apotome quadrangular, Fig. 48E), uniformly reddish-orange at earlier instars (ventral apotome triangular, Fig. 48F).
>
> Rivers, canals, streams and flowing marshes; among dense vegetation and roots. Widespread but local.

— Case strongly curved, with a smooth glossy appearance, composed of sand grains coated with secretion (Fig. 46F). 9th abdominal dorsum with 14 setae (Fig. 48B). Excluding anterior-lateral setal groups, mesodorsum with more than 10 setae (16–30 at instar V, ventral apotome quadrangular as in Fig. 48E) and metadorsum with more than 4 setae (11–13 at instar V)—   **Adicella filicornis** (Pictet)

> Head uniformly reddish-orange at all known instars.
>
> Very small, shallow springs. Extremely local; larval records from Devon, Gwynedd, Clwyd and Lanark District; old records of adults from Powys and Hampshire.

36(30) 3rd leg with two long setal fringes (Figs 48G, H); (fringes are sparse at instar II, Fig. 48I); larva readily swims. Case straight, composed of pieces of plant material, usually roots or filamentous leaves, arranged in a spiral (Fig. 49A)—   **37**

— 3rd leg without long setal fringes (Fig. 48J); larva does not swim. Case distinctly curved when small but almost straight when full-sized; composed of pieces of plant material, e.g. roots, arranged in two opposing spirals, one dextral and the other sinistral, which meet in a zig-zag line along the middle of the dorsal and ventral faces (Figs 49B, C)—   **Erotesis baltica** McLachlan

Head with a distinctive pattern (most obvious at instar V, Fig. 49D); subocular ecdysial line, present only at instar V, has a dorsal branch (arrow, Fig. 49D).

Dykes and lake fens; among roots. Rare; English Lake District, Cambridgeshire and Norfolk. Old records of adults from valleys of Rivers Test and Itchen (Hampshire).

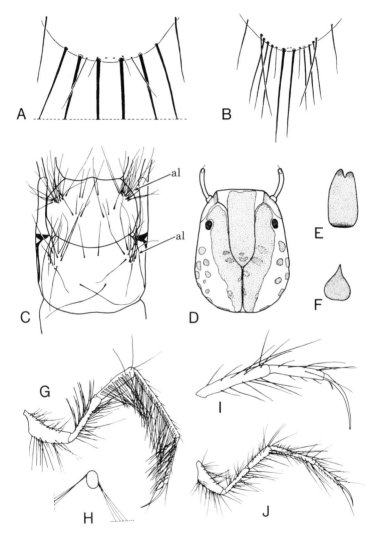

Fig. 48. **A, B**: part of 9th abdominal dorsum: A, *Adicella reducta*; B, *A. filicornis*. **C**: mesothorax and metathorax, dorsal view, of *A. reducta*. **D**: head capsule of *A. reducta*. **E, F**: ventral apotome of *A. reducta*: E, instar V; F, instar IV. **G, H**: 3rd leg of *Triaenodes bicolor*: G, posterior view; H, diagrammatic transverse section of tibia. **I**: tibia and tarsus of 3rd leg, anterior view, of *Ylodes conspersus*, instar II. **J**: 3rd leg, posterior view, of *Erotesis baltica*.

37 Tarsus of 3rd leg with 2 fringes of long setae, one *a* on anterior face, one *p* on posterior face (Fig. 49E); (anterior fringe is represented by only 1 or 2 long setae at instar II)—   **Triaenodes bicolor** (Curtis)

At instar V (ventral apotome quadrangular, Fig. 50A): ventral apotome is as pale or paler than adjoining parts of the genae (Fig. 50A); dorsal head pattern resembles Fig. 50D; 9th abdominal dorsum is dark grey-brown. At earlier instars (ventral apotome triangular, Fig. 50B) all sclerites are grey-brown.

Ponds, lakes and very slowly flowing canals and dykes; among vegetation. Widespread and common.

— Tarsus of 3rd leg with 1 fringe of long setae *p*, which arises on the posterior face (Fig. 49F)—   Genus YLODES, **38**

At instar V (ventral apotome quadrangular, Fig. 50C): ventral apotome is darker than adjoining parts of the genae (Fig. 50C); dorsal head pattern resembles Fig. 50E; 9th abdominal dorsum is straw to pale grey-brown. At earlier instars (ventral apotome triangular, as in Fig. 50B) all sclerites are pale brown. Not in static fresh water.

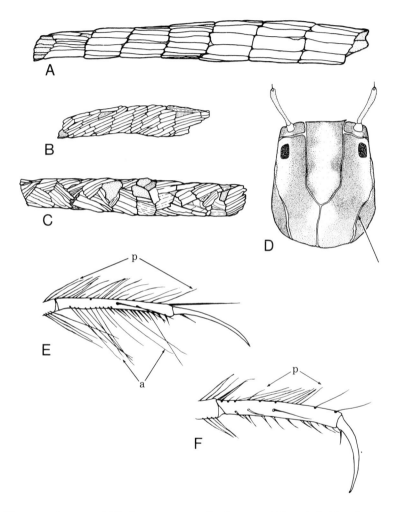

Fig. 49.   **A**: case of *Ylodes conspersus*.   **B, C**: case of *Erotesis baltica*: B, lateral view, instar IV; C, ventral view, instar V.   **D**: head capsule of *E. baltica*.   **E, F**: tarsus of 3rd leg, anterior view: E, *Triaenodes bicolor*; F, *Y. conspersus*.

38   Tarsus of 1st leg, in anterior view, with 1–3 short, pale setae on the
     ventral edge (arrows, Fig. 50F)—   **Ylodes conspersus** (Rambur)
                                                         Instars IV and V
           Rivers; among vegetation. Hereford and Worcester, and Dorset to
           Kent.

—   Tarsus of 1st leg, in anterior view, without setae on the ventral edge
     (Fig. 50G)—   **39**

39   Trochanter of 1st leg, in anterior view, with more than 2 short and
     pale ventral edge setae *ss* and more than 1 dorsal edge seta *ds* (Fig.
     50H)—   **Ylodes reuteri** (McLachlan)
                                    Instar V (and possibly earlier instars)
           Brackish water. Recorded from Orkney, Humberside, Suffolk,
           Essex, Kent and Co. Wexford.

—   Trochanter of 1st leg, in anterior view, with only 2 short and pale
     ventral edge setae *ss* and only 1 dorsal edge seta *ds* (as in Fig. 50I)—
                                                                      40

40   Ventral apotome quadrangular (as in Fig. 50C). Subocular ecdysial
     line *sl* present (as in Figs 50C, E)—   **Ylodes simulans** (Tjeder)
                                                                  Instar V
           Rivers; among vegetation. Recorded from Wales and River Forth.

—   Ventral apotome triangular (as in Fig. 50B). Subocular ecdysial line
     absent—   **Ylodes consperus** (Rambur)
                                                       Instars II and III
                                            Ylodes simulans (Tjeder)
                                                       Instars II to IV
                                and probably **Ylodes reuteri** (McLachlan)
                                                     Instars II, III, ? IV

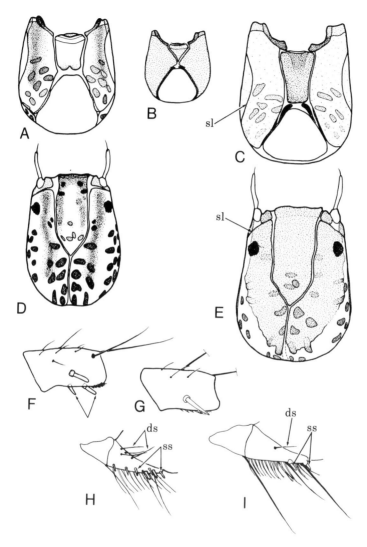

Fig. 50.   **A–C**: head capsule, ventral view: A, *Triaenodes bicolor*; B, *T. bicolor*,
instar IV; C, *Ylodes conspersus*.   **D, E**: head capsule: D, *T. bicolor*; E,
Y. conspersus.   **F, G**: tarsus of 1st leg, anterior view: F, *Y. conspersus*;
G, *Y. simulans*.   **H, I**: trochanter of 1st leg, anterior view: H, *Y. reuteri*;
I, *Y. conspersus*.

Family LIMNEPHILIDAE

The family Limnephilidae is the largest family of Trichoptera in the British Isles, with fifty-eight species in twenty-one genera (Table 8). It is a successful group, the larvae forming a conspicuous element of the fauna in a wide range of habitats. Many species have strategies which enable them to take advantage of waterbodies which only hold water from autumn to spring.

The family has no unique distinguishing feature and the larvae are rather similar to those of the family Lepidostomatidae. The arrangement of the dorsal thoracic sclerites (Fig. 1) distinguishes lepidostomatids and most limnephilids from other cased caddis (some limnephilids have modified or ill-defined metadorsal sclerites); all species have a prosternal horn (Fig. 2) and antennae which are set well back from the margin of the head capsule. Limnephilids differ from lepidostomatids in the presence of a dorsal protuberance on the first abdominal segment, the position of the antennae relative to the eye (Fig. 13A, except in the terrestrial *Enoicyla pusilla*) and the absence of a genal fold (Fig. 13B).

Plant litter derived from overhanging trees and emergent vegetation is the principal food source of most limnephilids; others eat living plants and algae while larvae with toothless mandibles scrape material from surfaces. The main growth period of those species which feed on plant litter falls between autumn and spring, when litter is most plentiful. Once the larvae are fully fed, they adopt one of two types of strategy. Some species enter a larval diapause and do not metamorphose until late summer or autumn; the larva may remain active or may fix its case ready for pupation, then spend several weeks inside as a larva. This group of species is restricted to permanent waterbodies and the females lay their eggs soon after emergence, under objects in or close to the water. In the other group of species, the larvae metamorphose in spring and the adults enter a diapause, not laying until summer or autumn. These species are able to utilize waterbodies which only hold water over winter (called 'temporary' waterbodies in the key). The eggs are laid in damp places, such as under logs on the otherwise dry bottom, and do not hatch until the waterbody floods, which may be several weeks later. This second group of species is also found abundantly in permanent waterbodies which diminish during summer, exposing margins with suitable egg-laying sites; the adults still emerge in spring. In contrast to these litter-feeding species, spring or summer is the main growth period of the comparatively few species which feed on living plants or algae.

TABLE 8.   HEAD WIDTHS OF LIMNEPHILIDAE
Ranges (and *n*) of head widths (mm) at instars III to V.

Species	Instar III	IV	V
Allogamus auricollis	0·45–0·56 (21)	0·77–0·95 (12)	1·07–1·42 (27)
Anabolia nervosa	—	0·86–1·03 (8)	1·17–1·57 (13)
Apatania auricula	—	0·60 (1)	0·77–0·84 (12)
A. muliebris	0·30–0·40 (3)	0·49–0·62 (8)	0·74–0·88 (20)
A. wallengreni	—	0·56–0·64 (12)	0·76–0·94 (14)
Chaetopteryx villosa	0·49–0·72 (12)	0·82–1·05 (20)	1·07–1·57 (85)
Drusus annulatus	0·56–0·58 (10)	0·86–0·96 (12)	1·21–1·56 (14)
Ecclisopteryx guttulata	0·56–0·60 (3)	0·88 (2)	1·38–1·44 (3)
Enoicyla pusilla[1]	0·50–0·60	0·64–0·79	0·77–0·98[2]
Glyphotaelius pellucidus	—	1·11–1·37 (6)	1·66–2·02 (15)
Grammotaulius nigro-punctatus	—	1·40–1·67 (15)	2·16–2·85 (21)
G. nitidus	—	—	—
Halesus digitatus	—	—	1·68–1·91 (24)
H. radiatus	—	—	1·58–2·03 (24)
H. radiatus/digitatus[3]	0·7–0·9 (62)	1·1–1·5 (115)	1·71–2·21 (132)
Hydatophylax infumatus	0·82 (1)	1·36, 1·42 (2)	1·84–2·24 (5)
Ironoquia dubia	—	—	1·44 (1)
Limnephilus affinis/incisus	—	0·66–0·88 (37)	0·99–1·33 (102)
L. auricula	—	0·73–0·81 (14)	0·93–1·22 (44)
L. binotatus	—	1·00–1·17 (11)	1·45–1·85 (32)
L. bipunctatus	—	1·02–1·17 (15)	1·38–1·71 (24)
L. borealis	—	1.12 (1)	1.34–1.71 (15)
L. centralis	—	0·72–0·86 (14)	0·90–1·26 (81)
L. coenosus	—	0·86–1·06 (18)	1·15–1·42 (42)
L. decipiens	—	0·90–1·06 (11)	1·20–1·62 (24)
L. elegans	—	1·24–1·37 (4)	1·72–2·03 (15)
L. extricatus	—	0·81–0·94 (10)	1·24–1·44 (48)
L. flavicornis	—	*1·06–1·27 (14)	1·43–1·91 (18)
L. fuscicornis	—	1·12–1·21 (3)	1·59–1·88 (14)
L. fuscinervis	—	—	1·48–1·58 (12)
L. griseus	—	0·91–1·07 (50)	1·24–1·46 (32)
L. hirsutus	—	0·77–0·94 (16)	1·13–1·37 (16)
L. ignavus	—	0·84–1·02 (39)	1·20–1·46 (25)

(Continued on p. 129)

TABLE 8. (continued)

Species	Instar III	IV	V
L. lunatus	—	0·83–0·99 (15)	1·26–1·56 (25)
L. luridus	—	0·96–1·13 (36)	1·33–1·68 (58)
L. marmoratus	—	*1·06–1·19 (13)	1·44–1·88 (22)
L. nigriceps	—	0·90–0·97 (16)	1·08–1·46 (44)
L. pati	—	—	—
L. politus	—	*1·06–1·26 (17)	1·44–1·88 (17)
L. rhombicus	—	*1·18–1·46 (11)	1·50–2·11 (34)
L. sparsus	—	0·94–1·17 (12)	1·24–1·44 (13)
L. stigma	—	*1·04–1·24 (10)	1·43–2·13 (20)
L. subcentralis	—	0·88–1·05 (8)	1·30–1·46 (15)
L. tauricus	—	—	—
L. vittatus	—	0·62–0·81 (11)	0·86–1·08 (25)
Melampophylax mucoreus	0·57–0·85 (8)	0·92–1·27 (16)	1·30–1·62 (25)
Mesophylax aspersus	—	—	1·15, 1·22 (2)
M. impunctatus	—	0·92 (1)	1·22–1·37 (12)
Micropterna lateralis	*0·81–0·94 (8)	1·12–1·42 (47)	1·55–2·07 (128)
M. sequax	*0·70–0·90 (18)	1·03–1·37 (62)	1·44–2·05 (327)
Nemotaulius punctatoli- neatus	—	1·43–1·57 (3)	2·27, 2·75 (2)
Phacopteryx brevipennis	—	0·95–1·06 (10)	1·24–1·48 (11)
Potamophylax cingulatus	—	—	1·62–2·20 (93)
P. latipennis	—	—	1·77–2·30 (109)
P. cingulatus/latipennis	0·79–0·95 (16)	1·13–1·45 (64)	—
P. rotundipennis	0·68–0·84 (11)	1·06–1·20 (14)	1·58–1·78 (23)
Rhadicoleptus alpestris	—	0·90–1·08 (13)	1·24–1·47 (7)
Stenophylax permistus	*0·81 (1)	1·37–1·53 (11)	1·67–2·21 (68)
S. vibex	*0·92–1·03 (21)	1·28–1·58 (27)	1·82–2·20 (49)

*Not keyed to species at this instar.

[1]Data from D. Harding (pers. comm.). Head width range at instar II is 0·38–0·46 mm.

[2]Dagger-like setae are present at the anterior-lateral corner of the pronotum at instar V only.

[3]Data from Garside (1979).

All limnephilids except *Limnephilus pati* are included in the key, though we have had to rely on foreign material or descriptions for two species, *Grammotaulius nitidus* and *Mesophylax aspersus*. *Limnephilus pati* and *L. tauricus* have only recently been recognized as distinct from *L. hirsutus* (O'Connor & Barnard 1981) and the larva of *L. pati* is completely unknown. There are old records of *L. pati* from fens and bogs in East Anglia, the Isle of Man and Ireland (O'Connor 1980) and in 1987 two males were light-trapped on the Isle of Man. Larvae of *Limnephilus affinis* cannot yet be separated from those of *L. incisus*.

A few points should be noted before proceeding with the key.

Primary and additional setae.   All first instar larvae have the same numbers of setae on the sclerites and leg sections. These are called primary setae. Additional (or secondary) setae appear at successive moults in different areas, depending on the species, and therefore are very useful in diagnosis.

Setae on the femora.   The primary setal arrangement of the femur (which is retained by many species at the second instar) is shown by Fig. 52F. Additional setae may arise along the dorsal or ventral edges (Figs 52G, 66A–F) or on the faces (*fs* in Figs 66A, B). Sometimes, the key refers to additional setae on a particular face (anterior or posterior). It is vital to look at the correct face. Two features readily distinguish them: the primary face seta lies closer to the ventral edge on the posterior face (Figs 66A, C) than on the anterior face (Figs 66B, D), and the proximal tip of the posterior face is hidden by the trochanter (part of the trochanter is shown in all figures of the femur in posterior view so that they are instantly recognizable).

Additional face setae may be difficult to see against the face of the femur, particularly if they are pale and fine. They are revealed in silhouette when the leg is viewed from above or below against background illumination. This method is also useful when investigating setae on other parts, e.g. the mesonotum.

Setae of the ninth abdominal dorsal sclerite. There are four long and four short primary setae. In many species the four long setae (*I* and *O*) remain very much the longest at all instars, e.g. Fig. 78C. In some species additional setae may develop to approach them in size (Figs 62A, D, 82C). Two conspicuous pits (*p* in Fig. 78C) are present on the sclerite of all species at all instars and should not be included in setal counts.

Problems caused by regeneration. Regeneration following injury to a leg segment or sclerite at an earlier instar can result in an abnormal setal arrangement at later instars. Short or mis-shapen legs or grossly distorted sclerites are obvious and must be ignored when identifying a larva. In addition, marked left/right asymmetry in setal sizes, particularly if any of the primary setae are involved, should also invite suspicion and suggest the omission of the abnormal part when keying the larva.

Colour patterning. Limnephilids are notable for their prominent muscle attachment spots. In pale larvae these are usually darker than the ground colour but in very dark larvae they may appear paler than the ground. Sometimes these muscle attachment spots have proved to be taxonomically significant, but unless specifically mentioned they are to be ignored and a description of the head as pale or dark refers to the ground colour.

It proved impossible to find unique combinations of characters which would allow every species to be keyed out only once; *Limnephilus binotatus* is particularly variable and appears several times in the key.

Key to larvae

1   Gills absent—   **2**

—   Gills present—   **3**

2   Antenna *a* situated very close to anterior margin of eye (Fig. 51A).
     Anal region with strong setae *ss* aligned parallel to the anal slit (Fig.
     51B). Larva terrestrial—   **Enoicyla pusilla** (Burmeister)

     Case conical, curved, of sand grains with fragments of dead leaves
     (Fig. 51C), sometimes entirely of leaf fragments when full-sized.

     Under dead oak leaves around grass tufts, and often in mouse or vole
     runs. Wyre Forest area of Hereford and Worcester.

—   Antenna *a* at least as close to anterior margin of head capsule as to
     eye (as in Fig. 55C). Anal region with strong setae *ss* aligned transverse
     to the anal slit (Fig. 51D). Larva aquatic—
                                     Instar II of species which have only
                                     single-filament gills at instars III to V
                                     (not keyed out further)

3(1) All gills consist of single filaments only (Fig. 51E); (look particu-
     larly at the ventral gills on abdominal segments 2 and 3; included in
     this group is *Apatania* in which two single gill filaments may arise very
     close together at the anterior-dorsal position on abdominal segments 2
     and 3, Figs 54D, E)—   **5**

—   Some gills consist of more than 1 filament (Fig. 51F)—   **4**

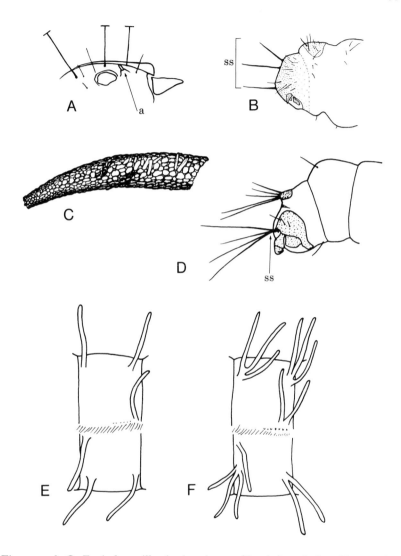

Fig. 51.   **A–C**: *Enoicyla pusilla*: A, dorsal part of head, lateral view; B, posterior end of abdomen, lateral view; C, case.   **D**: posterior end of abdomen of *Potamophylax* sp., instar II, lateral view.   **E, F**: 3rd abdominal segment, lateral view: E, *Potamophylax latipennis*; F, *Anabolia nervosa*.

4 Gills consist of up to 2 filaments only—

      Instar III of species which have some gills with three or more filaments at instars IV and V (not keyed out further)

— Some gills consist of 3 or more filaments—   **31**

5(3) Larva with ANY of the following features:
  (a) Metadorsum with 1 seta on each anterior-median sclerite *a* (Fig. 52A).
  (b) Metadorsum with 3 setae on each posterior sclerite *p* (Figs 52A, B).
  (c) 1st abdominal dorsum with 5 setae on each side, arranged as in Fig. 52D: 1 lateral *ls*, 1 anterior-median *as*, and 3 posterior *ps* (2 of which may be very small).
  (d) Femur of 2nd leg with only 2 setae on the dorsal edge (arrows, Fig. 52F)—

      Instar II of species which have some multi-filament gills at instars III to V; also *Stenophylax permistus* (not keyed out further)

— Larva with ALL of the following features:
  (a) Metadorsum with more than 1 seta on each anterior-median sclerite *a* (Figs 52C, 53A).
  (b) Metadorsum with more than 3 setae on each posterior sclerite *p* (Figs 52C, 53A).
  (c) 1st abdominal dorsum with more than 5 setae on each side (Fig. 52E).
  (d) Femur of 2nd leg with more than 2 setae on the dorsal edge (Figs 52G, 57G)—   **6**

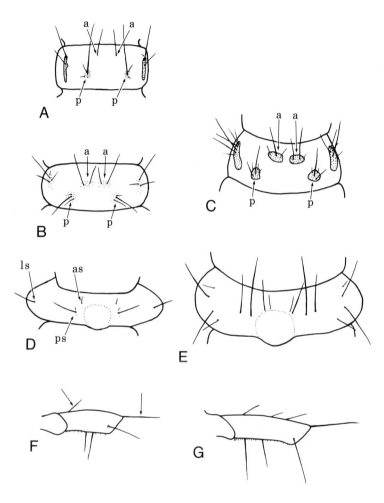

Fig. 52. **A–C**: metadorsum: A, *Limnephilus* sp., instar II; B, *Limnephilus ?luridus*, instar II; C, *Halesus* sp., instar III.   **D, E**: 1st abdominal segment, dorsal view: D, *L.?flavicornis*, instar II; E, *Halesus* sp. instar III. **F, G**: femur of 2nd leg, posterior view: F, *L. ?affinis*, instar II; G, *Chaetopteryx villosa*, instar III.

6   Metadorsum with one or more obvious anterior-median sclerites *a*
    from which most setae of that area arise (Figs 53A, 55D). Lateral
    fringe *f* absent from anterior half of 2nd abdominal segment (Fig.
    53C; setae *lls* are not part of the fringe)—   **10**

—   Metadorsum without obvious anterior-median sclerites though two
    groups of prominent setae *as* are present (Fig. 53B). Lateral fringe *f*
    present on anterior half of 2nd abdominal segment (Figs 54D–F)—
                                          Genus APATANIA, **7**

        Mandibles lack teeth and ridges (as in Figs 56C, E). Case curved, of
        small mineral particles (Figs 53D, E).

7   Head width 0·56–0·64 mm (instar IV) or 0·75–0·94 mm (instar V)—
                                                                8

—   Head width less than 0·50 mm—   APATANIA spp.
                                    Instar III (not keyed out further)

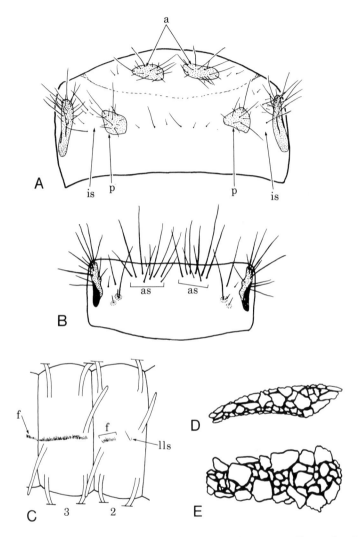

Fig. 53. **A, B**: metadorsum: A, *Halesus* sp.; B, *Apatania wallengreni*.   **C**: 2nd and 3rd abdominal segments, lateral view, of *Potamophylax latipennis*. **D, E**: case of *Apatania muliebris*: D, lateral view; E, dorsal view.

8   Setae of anterior edge of pronotum with long, tapering, somewhat
    flexuous tips (Fig. 54B; those shown are in region *R*, Fig. 54A). 1st
    abdominal segment with 14–27 dorsal setae on each side at instar V,
    8–10 at instar IV; at instar V the most ventro-lateral seta of the group,
    vs, is ventral to the base of the posterior-dorsal gill *pdg* of the segment,
    if that gill is present (Fig. 54D)— **Apatania muliebris** McLachlan
                                                    Instars IV and V

> Head predominantly brown with a slightly paler area in the centre of
> the posterior half of the fronto-clypeal apotome (Fig. 55A); posterior-
> lateral muscle attachment spots slightly paler than adjacent area of
> gena though they have dark outlines.
>
> Small streams and trickles, apparently always near springs; stony
> substratum. Widespread but very local.

—   Setae of anterior edge of pronotum sword- or dagger-shaped, never
    with long tapering tips (Fig. 54C). 1st abdominal segment with 4–10
    dorsal setae on each side at instar V (Figs 54E, F), 4–6 at instar IV;
    at instar V the most ventro-lateral seta of the group, *vs*, is dorsal to
    the base of the posterior-dorsal gill *pdg* of the segment, if that gill is
    present (Fig. 54E)—   **9**

9   Anal proleg lateral sclerite with 6–8 setae *ps* along the posterior edge
    at instar V (Fig. 54G), 5–7 at instar IV (look at both prolegs). 9th
    abdominal dorsum with 36–47 setae *ds* at instar V (Fig. 54G), 21–26
    at instar IV. 2nd abdominal segment with 1 anterior-dorsal gill *adg*
    on each side (Fig. 54F); 1st abdominal segment without posterior-
    dorsal gills (Fig. 54F)—   **Apatania wallengreni** McLachlan
                                                    Instars IV and V

> Head predominantly pale yellow with irregular grey-brown areas and
> very dark posterior-lateral muscle attachment spots at instar V (Fig.
> 55C), overally darker at instar IV.
>
> Lake shores; stony substratum. Scotland, English Lake District,
> Llyn Tegid (Gwynedd) and western Ireland; locally common.

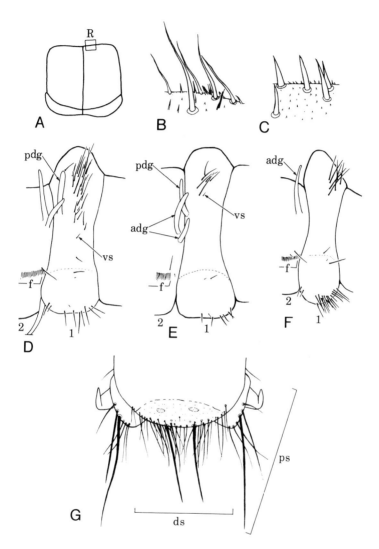

Fig. 54.   **A**: outline of head and pronotum, lateral view, of *Apatania* sp.   **B, C**:
anterior edge of pronotum in region *R* of Fig. 54A: B, *Apatania muliebris*;
C, *A. wallengreni*.   **D–F**: 1st abdominal segment and anterior part of
2nd, lateral view: D, *A. muliebris*; E, *A. auricula*; F, *A.
wallengreni*.   **G**: 9th abdominal segment, dorsal view, of *A. wallengreni*.

— Anal proleg lateral sclerite with only 5 setae along the posterior edge. 9th abdominal dorsum with 21–26 setae at instar V, about 17 at instar IV. 2nd abdominal segment with 2 anterior-dorsal gills *adg* on each side at instar V (Fig. 54E), 1 at instar IV; 1st abdominal segment usually with posterior-dorsal gill *pdg* (Fig. 54E)—

Apatania auricula (Forsslund)
Instars IV and V

Head similar to that of *A. muliebris* but has a paler posterior-lateral region with dark muscle attachment spots (Fig. 55B).

Lake shores; stony substratum. South-west Ireland only; abundant.

10(6) Metadorsum with 1 central anterior-median sclerite *a* (Fig. 55D). 1st abdominal venter with two large median sclerites *m*, each bearing several setae (Fig. 55E)— **Hydatophylax infumatus** (McLachlan)

Femora of 2nd and 3rd legs without additional proximo-dorsal or face setae (as in Fig. 57G). 2nd abdominal segment lacks anterior gills. Case resembles Figs 58A, B, but is composed of dead wood at instar V.

Among woody debris (on which the larvae feed); usually in flowing water. Widespread; never abundant.

— Metadorsum with 2 anterior-median sclerites *a* (Fig. 53A). 1st abdominal venter without large median sclerites (Fig. 55F)— **11**

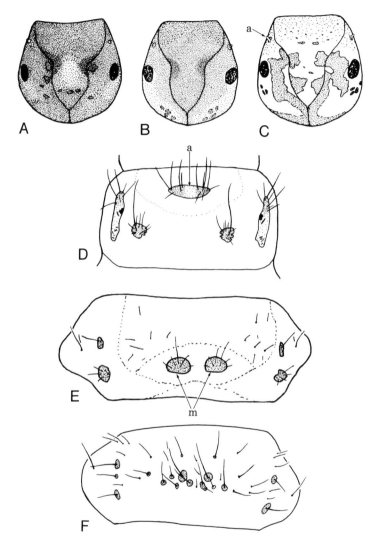

Fig. 55. **A–C**: head capsule: A, *Apatania muliebris*; B, *A. auricula*; C, *A. wallengreni*. **D**: metathorax, dorsal view, of *Hydatophylax infumatus*. **E, F**: 1st abdominal segment, ventral view: E, *H. infumatus*; F, *Allogamus auricollis*.

11   Mandibles with teeth along edges (Fig. 56A) and with ridges in central
     concavity; (teeth may be best seen from in front, Fig. 56B)—   **14**

—   Mandibles without teeth along edges (Figs 56C, E), except that one
     tooth *t* may be present on dorsal edge (Fig. 56D); central concavity
     without ridges—   **12**

12   Femora with additional setae *fs* on the faces (as in Figs 61D–L). 1st
     abdominal lateral protuberance without a posterior sclerite but with
     anterior setae *aps* at a median position (Figs 56F, G); (at instar V the
     setae form a conspicuous band but at instar III only 1 or 2 are
     present)—   **13**

     Case curved, of mineral particles at all instars (Fig. 56H).

—   All femora without additional setae on the faces (as in Figs 57E–G).
     1st abdominal lateral protuberance with a posterior sclerite *s* but
     without anterior setae at a median position (as in Figs 59C, D)—
                         Melampophylax mucoreus (Hagen)

     All sclerites dark brown or black. Case curved, composed mainly
     of mineral particles at instar V but plant fragments occasionally
     predominate at instar III.

     Streams and rivers, one lake shore (Malham Tarn, Yorkshire); stony
     substratum; commonest in alkaline waters. England, Wales and
     southern Scotland; may be locally abundant.

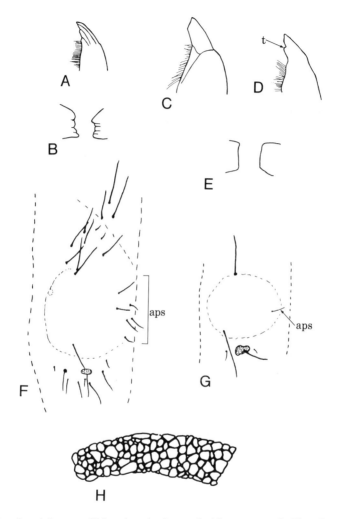

Fig. 56. **A**: right mandible, dorsal view, of *Allogamus auricollis*. **B**: worn mandibles of *Potamophylax cingulatus* viewed from in front. **C, D**: right mandible, dorsal view: C, *Drusus annulatus*; D, *Melampophylax mucoreus*. **E**: worn mandibles of *M. mucoreus* viewed from in front. **F, G**: 1st abdominal segment, lateral region, of *D. annulatus*: F, instar V; G, instar III. **H**: case of *D. annulatus*.

13   Parietal with a group of pale setae *ps* between the eye and the fronto-clypeal apotome (Fig. 57A); (these setae are very obvious at instar V but are not conspicuous at instar III; those close to the fronto-clypeal apotome are easiest to see, Fig. 57B)—

Ecclisopteryx guttulata (Pictet)

Head yellow brown at instars IV and V, darker at instar III. Head and pronotum without conspicuous surface sculpturing.

Large streams and rivers; stony substratum. Locally common in northern and western Britain; also recorded from eastern Ireland.

—   Parietal without a group of pale setae between the eye and the fronto-clypeal apotome (Fig. 57C)—   **Drusus annulatus** Stephens

Head dark brown at all instars. Head and pronotum with conspicuous granular surface sculpturing (Fig. 57D).

Usually in streams, less common in rivers, rare on lake shores; stony substratum and among weeds. Widespread and common.

14(11) At least one femur of the 2nd and 3rd legs with one or more setae *pds* **proximal** to the large primary proximal seta *pps* on the dorsal edge (Figs 57E, F)—   Genus HALESUS, **15**

Instars IV, V and most of instar III

Mesopleurite ventral process *vp* without setae (Fig. 57H). Case composed of large plant fragments (Figs 58A, B); cases solely of mineral material are rare.

—   No femur of the 2nd and 3rd legs with any setae **proximal** to the large primary seta *pps* on the dorsal edge (Fig. 57G)—   **18**

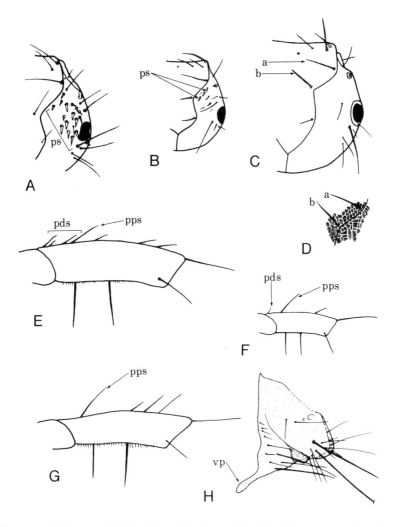

Fig. 57. **A, B**: part of right side of head capsule of *Ecclisopteryx guttulata*: A, instar V; B, instar III. **C**: part of right side of head capsule of *Drusus annulatus*. **D**: surface sculpturing of head of *D. annulatus* in the area of setae *a* and *b*, Fig. 57C. **E–G**: femur of 2nd leg, posterior view: E, *Halesus* sp., instar V; F, *Halesus* sp., instar III; G, *Chaetopteryx villosa*. **H**: mesopleurite of *Halesus* sp..

15 Anterior-lateral region of head with a clear pale patch (arrow, Fig.
    58C)—   **Halesus radiatus** (Curtis)
                                        Instars III to V (most key out here)

    Case tube usually rough in outline (Figs 58A, B), not made entirely
    of butted fragments; long sticks may be added.

    Streams, rivers and lake shores; infrequent in very small streams.
    Widespread and common.

—   Anterior-lateral region of head either without a pale patch or with an
    indistinct patch of dark and pale flecks—   **16**

16 Head width more than 1·60 mm—   **17**

—   Head width less than 1·60 mm—   **Halesus digitatus** (Schrank)
                                                Instars III and IV
                                           Halesus radiatus (Curtis)
                                              Instars III and IV (some)

17 Note: Larvae which do not fall easily into either category cannot be
    identified.
    Posterior region of fronto-clypeal apotome with both sides generally
    diverging from the mid-line for some distance in front of the posterior
    setae *ps*, so that its widest part *w* lies anterior to setae *ps* (Fig. 58D)—
                                           Halesus radiatus (Curtis)
                                                     Instar V (some)

    See couplet 15 for case and habitat.

—   Posterior region of fronto-clypeal apotome with both sides generally
    converging towards the mid-line for some distance in front of the
    posterior setae *ps*, so that its widest part *w* lies at the level of setae *ps*
    (Fig. 58E)—   **Halesus digitatus** (Schrank)
                                                        Instar V

    Case frequently a smooth tube of butted plant fragments (as in Fig.
    61C) with or without added long sticks.

    Streams and rivers; commoner than *H. radiatus* in small streams, less
    frequent than *H. radiatus* in rivers. Widespread and common.

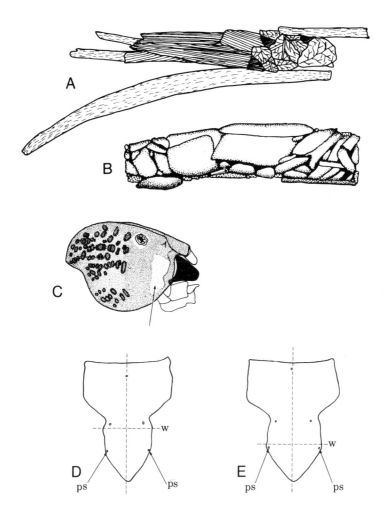

Fig. 58. **A**: case of *Halesus* sp., instar III.   **B**: case of *Halesus radiatus*.   **C**: head, lateral view, of *H. radiatus*.   **D, E**: fronto-clypeal apotome (line from apex to median pit *mp* is the mid-line): D, *H. radiatus*; E, *H. digitatus*.

18(14) 1st abdominal lateral protuberance with anterior setae *aps* at a
        median position (Figs 59A, B); (at instar V the setae form a conspicu-
        ous band but at instar III only 1 or 2 are present)—
                                            Allogamus auricollis (Pictet)

> All sclerites dark brown or black. 9th abdominal dorsal sclerite with
> 2 central intermediate setae *C* (Fig. 59E); the anterior intermediate
> setae *A* are shorter than setae *C* (Fig 59E). Mesopleurite ventral
> process *vp* with at least 1 seta (as in Fig. 62E). Case long and narrow,
> composed entirely of small mineral particles (Fig. 59F) except at
> instar III when a few plant fragments may be incorporated.
>
> Large streams and rivers; stony substratum. Scotland and northern
> England; may be locally abundant. Welsh status uncertain.

—   1st abdominal lateral protuberance without anterior setae at a median
    position (Figs 59C, D)—   **19**

19 Posterior region of 1st abdominal lateral protuberance with a large
    sclerite *s* which lacks setae but has 1-3, usually 2, holes (Figs 59C,
    D); (sclerite may be very pale, particularly in small larvae, but its
    smooth shiny surface will distinguish it from the surrounding cuticle).
    Femora of 2nd and 3rd legs never with additional setae on the faces
    (as in Fig. 57G)—   **25**

—   Posterior region of 1st abdominal lateral protuberance either without
    a sclerite (Fig. 60A) or with 1–3 small separate sclerites *s* which lack
    setae but have a large central hole (Fig. 60B). Femora of 2nd and 3rd
    legs may have additional setae *fs* on the faces (Figs 61D–L)—   **20**

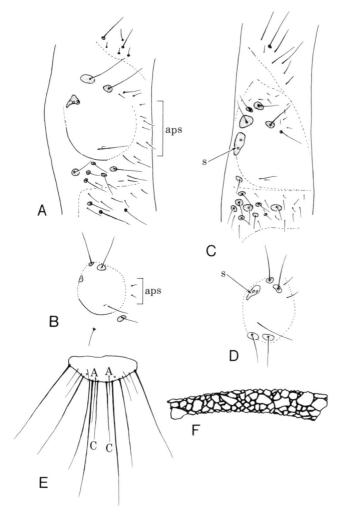

Fig. 59. **A–D**: 1st abdominal segment, lateral region: A, *Allogamus auricollis*, instar V; B, *A. auricollis*, instar III; C, *Potamophylax cingulatus*, instar V; D, *Potamophylax* sp., instar III. **E**: 9th abdominal dorsal sclerite of *A. auricollis*. **F**: case of *A. auricollis*.

20   Head with spinules restricted to a small patch *sp* behind the eye
     (Fig. 60C); (spinules appear as tiny dark points at ×50 to ×100
     magnification but at ×400 are seen to be conical outgrowths of the
     cuticle, *p* in Fig. 60D; the spinules may lie under a deposit of silt,
     which should be removed)—   Genus STENOPHYLAX, **21**

> *Stenophylax* species are not separable at instar III: head width less
> than 1·20 mm.
>
> Case straight, of butted leaf fragments (Fig. 61A).

—   Head with spinules over most of the dorsal surface of the parietal and
     often also on the fronto-clypeal apotome (Fig. 60E); (spinules in area
     sp may be slightly more prominent than those elsewhere—
                                        Genus MICROPTERNA, **24**

> *Micropterna* species are not separable at instar III: head width less
> than 1·00 mm.
>
> Case almost always slightly curved, of mineral particles and/or butted
> leaf fragments (Figs 61B, C).

21   Additional setae *fs* (Fig. 61D) present on the anterior face of at least
     three of the four femora of the 2nd and 3rd legs—
                         Stenophylax permistus McLachlan
                                   Instars IV (most) and V

> Length *l* of femur★ of 2nd leg (Fig. 61D) at least twice the width of
> labrum.
>
> ★NOTE: Both left and right femora should be measured and then
> averaged, unless one is malformed.
>
> Temporary, slow-flowing ditches and runnels under deciduous trees.
> Widespread and common.

—   Additional setae absent from the anterior face of at least three of the
     four femora of the 2nd and 3rd legs—   **22**

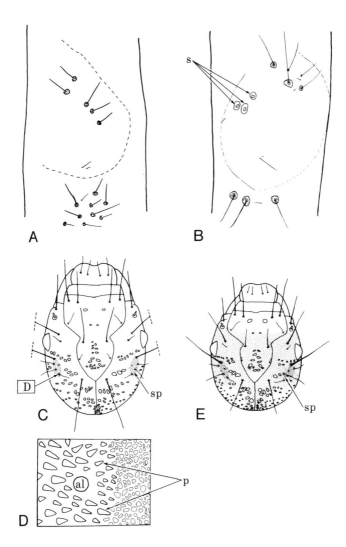

Fig. 60. **A, B**: 1st abdominal segment, lateral region: A, *Micropterna sequax*; B, *Stenophylax permistus*. **C**: head of *S. vibex*. **D**: detail of edge of spinule patch of *S. vibex*, area arrowed in Fig. 60C (*al* = setal alveolus). **E**: head of *M. sequax*.

22   Head width more than 1·60 mm—   **Stenophylax vibex** (Curtis)
                                                    Instar V

       Length l of femur of 2nd leg (see Fig. 61D) usually less than twice
       width of labrum (see note above*).

       Temporary, often fast-flowing runnels in deciduous woodland.
       Throughout Britain, but local.

—   Head width less than 1·60 mm—   **23**

23   Length l of femur of 2nd leg (see Fig. 61D) at least 2·03 times width
    of labrum (see note above*)—   **Stenophylax permistus** McLachlan
                                                    Instar IV (some)

       See couplet 21 for habitat.

—   Length of femur of 2nd leg less than 2·03 times width of labrum—
                                            Stenophylax vibex (Curtis)
                                                    Instar IV

       See couplet 22 for habitat.

24(20) Posterior faces of femora of 2nd and 3rd legs with additional
    setae fs confined to the ventral third, and typically with at least one
    row of three fs (Figs 61E–H)—   **Micropterna sequax** McLachlan
                                                    Instars IV and V

       At instar V, length l of femur of 2nd leg (see Fig. 61D and note* to
       couplet 21) is in the range of head width (w) + 0·14 mm to w − 0·09
       mm; at instar IV, l is usually in the range of w − 0·09 mm to w −
       0·19 mm. Case curved, usually of small mineral particles when full-
       sized (Fig. 61B) but fragments of dead leaves sometimes predominate.

       Small, semi-permanent or permanent streams. Widespread and
       common.

—   Posterior faces of femora of 2nd and 3rd legs with additional setae fs
    not confined to the ventral third, or with only one fs or none (Figs
    61I–L)—   **Micropterna lateralis** (Stephens)
                                                    Instars IV and V

       At instar V, length l of femur of 2nd leg (see Fig. 61D and note* to
       couplet 21) is at least 0·10 mm less than the head width; at instar
       IV, l is at least 0·20 mm less. Case usually curved, occasionally
       almost straight, of fragments of dead leaves when full-sized (Fig.
       61C) though small mineral particles sometimes predominate.

       Small, temporary streams and ditches. Widespread and common.

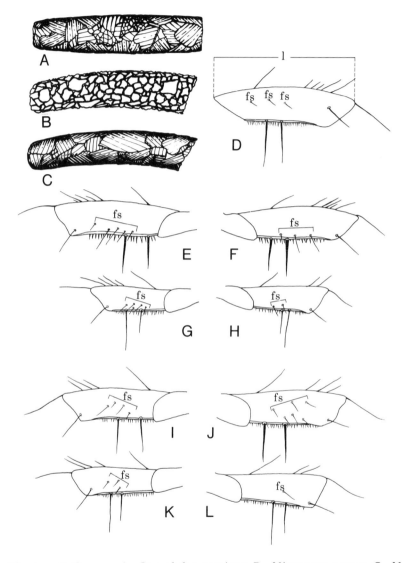

Fig. 61. **A–C**: case: A, *Stenophylax permistus*; B, *Micropterna sequax*; C, *M. lateralis*. **D**: femur of 2nd leg, anterior view, of *S. permistus*. **E–H**: femora of *M. sequax*, posterior views: E, F, 2nd legs; G, H, 3rd legs. **I–L**: femora of *M. lateralis*, posterior views: I, J, 2nd legs; K, L, 3rd legs.

25(19) 9th abdominal dorsal sclerite with both anterior intermediate
setae *A* as long as or longer than both of the central intermediate setae
C (Fig. 62A); (this feature is best seen from the side, Fig. 62B; Fig.
62C should help to identify the setae)—   **26**
                    (*Potamophylax cingulatus* and *P. latipennis.*
                    These are not separable at instars
                    III and IV: head width less than 1·50 mm)

> 9th abdominal dorsum with at least 2 posterior-lateral setae *pls* on
> each side at instars IV and V (Fig. 62A) and sometimes at instar III.
> Except at instar III, 1st abdominal dorsum has at least 4 setae *ps*
> posterior to the protuberance *pr* (Fig. 64B). Mesopleurite ventral
> process *vp* with at least 1 seta (Fig. 62E). Sclerites of metadorsum
> and 1st abdominal lateral protuberance brown. Case of mineral
> particles when full-sized (Fig. 64A); smaller cases include plant
> material and one form resembles the case of *Glyphotaelius pellucidus*
> shown in Figs 69D–F.

— 9th abdominal dorsal sclerite with both anterior intermediate setae *A*
shorter than the one or two central intermediate setae *C* (Fig. 62D)—
                    27

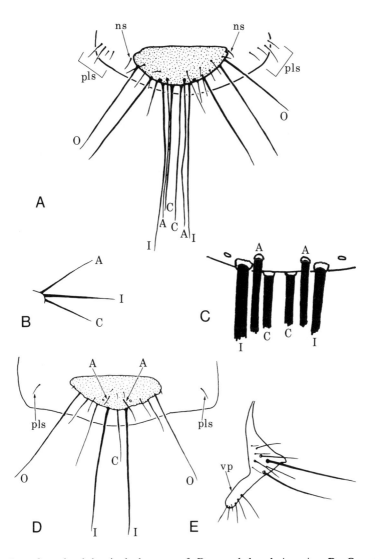

Fig. 62. **A**: 9th abdominal dorsum of *Potamophylax latipennis*. **B, C**: 9th abdominal dorsal sclerite of *P. latipennis*, central region of posterior edge: B, lateral view; C, dorsal view. **D**: 9th abdominal dorsum of *Chaetopteryx villosa*. **E**: mesopleurite, ventral portion, of *P. latipennis*.

26   Pale patch present between the eye and the nearest muscle attachment spots *m* posterior to it (area 2 in Figs 63A–C)*—

Potamophylax cingulatus (Stephens)

Instar V

The coloration of the head varies considerably and a pattern of pale areas may be more or less extensive; occasionally the band consisting of areas 1–4 (Figs 63A, B) occupies most of the lateral region of the head.

Streams and rivers, also occasionally lake shores; stony substratum. Widespread and common.

—   No pale patch between the eye and the nearest muscle attachment spots *m* posterior to it (Fig. 63F)*—

Potamophylax latipennis (Curtis)

Instar V

Head uniformly dark brown except for area 4 which is often slightly paler (Figs 63D, E).

Streams, rivers and lake shores; stony substratum. Widespread and common. In river systems, *P. latipennis* and *P. cingulatus* often occur together, *P. cingulatus* predominating in the upper reaches while *P. latipennis* is the commoner lower down.

* This character has been tested with a large number of specimens from many areas of the British Isles; recently, a few *P. latipennis* with a pale area 2 have been found in Caithness.

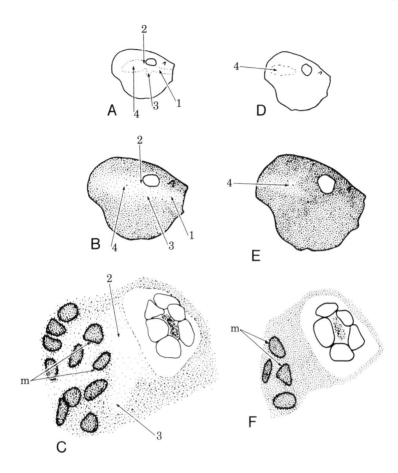

Fig. 63. **A–C**: head capsule of *Potamophylax cingulatus*: A, B, lateral view; C, eye and region immediately posterior to it. **D–F**: head capsule of *P. latipennis*: D, E, lateral view; F, eye and region immediately posterior to it.

27(25) 9th abdominal dorsum with at least 2 posterior-lateral setae *pls* on each side (as in Fig. 62A); (do not include any seta *ns* which arises very close to the sclerite)— **Potamophylax rotundipennis** (Brauer) Instars IV (some) and V

> Sclerites of metadorsum and 1st abdominal lateral protuberance pale straw in colour. Metadorsum usually with 1 or more setae *is* on the soft cuticle between the posterior and lateral sclerites (as in Fig. 53A). 1st abdominal dorsum may have up to 8 setae *ps* posterior to the protuberance *pr* (see Fig. 64B). 9th abdominal dorsal sclerite frequently with 2 central intermediate setae *C* (as in Fig. 59E). Case typically of sand grains, with a distinctive shape when full-sized (Fig. 65A).

> Streams and small rivers; sandy substratum with stones. Throughout England, but very local; also an old record from Lanark District. Usually found in small numbers.

— 9th abdominal dorsum with only 1 posterior-lateral seta *pls* on each side (Fig. 62D); (ensure that no small, pale seta has been overlooked)—   **28**

28 Head width more than 1·05 mm—   **29**

— Head width less than 1·05 mm—   **30**

29 Sclerites of metadorsum and 1st abdominal lateral protuberance brown in colour—   **Chaetopteryx villosa** (Fabricius) Instar V

> Metadorsum usually without setae on the soft cuticle between the posterior and lateral sclerites (as in Fig. 52C). 1st abdominal dorsum rarely with more than 2 setae *ps* posterior to the protuberance *pr* (Fig. 64C). 9th abdominal dorsal sclerite rarely with more than 1 central intermediate seta *C* (Fig. 62D). Case curved, rough in outline, of mineral particles with some plant fragments.

> Streams, also rivers and small upland lakes; stony and weedy substrata. Widespread and common.

— Sclerites of metadorum and 1st abdominal lateral protuberance pale straw in colour—   **Potamophylax rotundipennis** (Brauer) Instar IV (some)

> See couplet 27 for further information.

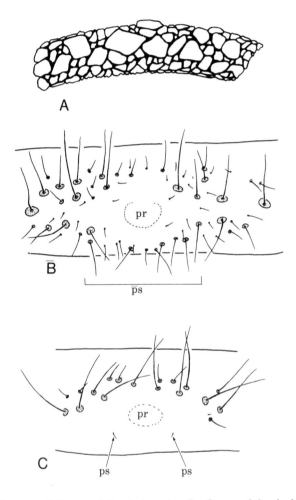

Fig. 64. **A**: case of *Potamophylax latipennis*. **B, C**: 1st abdominal segment, dorsal region: B, *P. latipennis*; C, *Chaetopteryx villosa*.

30(28) Note: Larvae which do not fall easily into any of the three
categories below cannot be identified.

1st abdominal lateral protuberance with a dark posterior sclerite s
which is similar in colour to the pigmented areas at the bases of setae
on the protuberance (as in Fig. 59D). Case shaggy, composed of plant
fragments (Fig. 65B). Larva found in spring (or throughout the year
at high altitudes)—   **Chaetopteryx villosa** (Fabricius)
                                                  Instars III and IV

    See couplet 29 for habitat.

— 1st abdominal lateral protuberance with a very pale posterior sclerite
which is paler than the pigmented areas at the bases of setae on the
protuberance. Case of plant material with one or more long pieces
which over-reach its posterior end (Fig. 58A). Larva found in winter
and spring—   **Halesus digitatus** (Schrank)
                                        Halesus radiatus (Curtis)
                                                  Instar III (some)

    See couplets 15 and 19 for habitats.

— 1st abdominal lateral protuberance with the posterior sclerite and all
areas at the bases of setae pale straw in colour. Case curved, made of
sand grains with only small plant fragments incorporated. Larva
found in autumn—   **Potamophylax rotundipennis** (Brauer)
                                                  Instar III

    See couplet 27 for habitat.

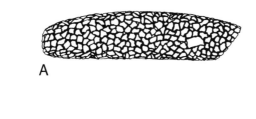

A

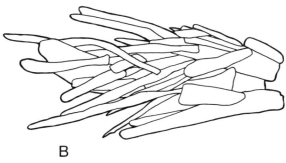

B

Fig. 65. **A**: case of *Potamophylax rotundipennis*. **B**: case of *Chaetopteryx villosa*, instar III.

31(4) At least one femur of the 2nd and 3rd legs with one or more additional setae *fs* on either the anterior or posterior face (Figs 66A, B); (if complement of additional 'face' setae is a single seta lying distally on, or very close to, the ventral edge of one femur, follow the second part of this couplet)—   **32**

—   No femur of the 2nd and 3rd legs with any additional setae on the faces (Figs 66C, D)—   **54**

32   Femur of 2nd leg with 2 strong ventral edge setae *vs* (Figs 66A, B, E); (one or more slender setae *ss* may also be present on or near the edge (Fig. 66E)—   **35**

—   Femora of both 2nd legs with 3 or more strong ventral edge setae *vs* (Fig. 66F)—   **33**

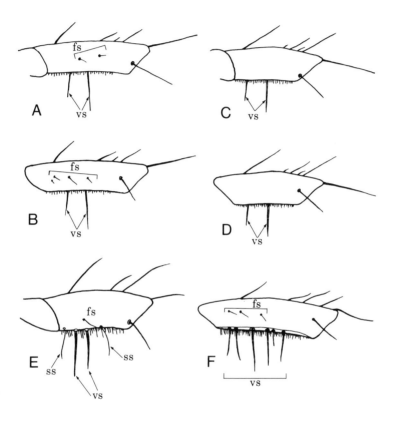

Fig. 66. **A, B**: femur of 2nd leg of *Limnephilus affinis*: A, posterior view; B, anterior view. **C, D**: femur of 2nd leg of *L. sparsus*: C, posterior view; D, anterior view. **E**: femur of 2nd leg, posterior view, of *L. hirsutus*. **F**: femur of 2nd leg, anterior view, of *Mesophylax impunctatus*.

33 Gills consist of up to 4 filaments. Metaventer with setae *ms* in addition to the four primary setae *ps* (Fig. 67A)—

Genus MESOPHYLAX, **34**

Head without bands, though fronto-clypeal apotome has a dark mark (Fig. 67B). Case slightly curved, usually of small mineral particles (as in Fig. 61B).

— Some gills consist of 5 or more filaments (Fig. 67C). Metaventer with only the four primary setae—   **Ironoquia dubia** (Stephens)

Head with wide brown bands; pronotum and mesonotum with a broad pale stripe along the mid-line (Figs 67D, E). Femur of 1st leg with 3 ventral edge setae *vs* (Fig. 67F). Case strongly curved, of butted leaf fragments (Fig. 67G).

Small, shallow streams in deciduous woods. South-east and eastern England; rare.

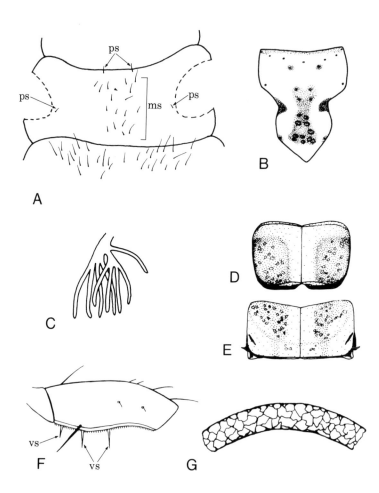

Fig. 67. **A**: metaventer and part of 1st abdominal venter of *Mesophylax impunctatus*. **B**: fronto-clypeal apotome of *M. aspersus*. **C–G**: *Iron-oquia dubia*: C, gill; D, pronotum; E, mesonotum; F, femur of 1st leg, posterior view; G, case.

34   Femur of 1st leg with 2 ventral edge setae *vs* (as in Fig. 68B)—
                            Mesophylax impunctatus McLachlan

       Exposed lake shores, under stones on gravel. Scotland, northern
       England and south-west Ireland.

—   Femora of both 1st legs with 3 ventral edge setae *vs* (as in Fig. 67F)—
                            Mesophylax aspersus (Rambur)

       (Based on foreign material and a description by Botosaneanu 1974).

       Streams. Occasional records of adults in southern England; no larvae
       have been found in the British Isles; the species may not breed here
       (Kimmins 1963).

35(32) Femur of 1st leg with ventral edge setae *vs* contrasting in colour,
       the distal seta being dark and the proximal seta pale (Fig. 68A)—
                                                                36

—   Femur of 1st leg with both ventral edge setae *vs* pale in colour (Fig.
       68B)—   37

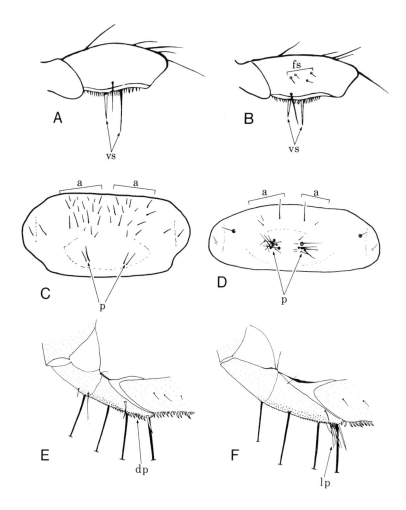

Fig. 68. **A, B**: femur of 1st leg, posterior view: A, *Glyphotaelius pellucidus*; B, *Anabolia nervosa*. **C, D**: 1st abdominal venter: C, *Phacopteryx brevipennis*; D, *G. pellucidus*. **E, F**: trochanter of 2nd leg, anterior view: E, *P. brevipennis*; F, *G. pellucidus*.

36 Femur of 1st leg with additional setae *fs* on anterior and/or posterior
    faces (as in Fig. 68B). 1st abdominal venter with more setae in the
    anterior groups *a* than in the posterior groups *p* (Fig. 68C); no seta
    in these groups arises from a pigmented area—
                                  Phacopteryx brevipennis (Curtis)

> Head mainly dark brown, sometimes with posterior tip of fronto-
> clypeal apotome slightly paler (as in Fig. 80D). Distal region of
> trochanters of 2nd and 3rd legs with a ventral row of stout dagger-
> like spines *dp* and no, or few, long flexuous spines (Fig. 68E). Case
> straight, triangular in cross-section, made of disks cut from dead
> leaves (Figs 69A–C).

> Shallow, usually temporary, pools in fens where there is a very slight
> water flow; usually under deciduous trees. South-west Scotland,
> England and Ireland; very local.

— Femur of 1st leg without additional setae on the faces (Fig. 68A). 1st
    abdominal venter with fewer setae in the anterior groups *a* than in
    the posterior groups *p* (Fig. 68D); some setae in these groups arise
    from individual small pigmented areas—
                                  Glyphotaelius pellucidus (Retzius)

> Head brown, usually with small pale patches around edges of fronto-
> clypeal apotome (Fig. 69G). Distal region of trochanters of 2nd and
> 3rd legs with a ventral row of long flexuous spines *lp* and no, or few,
> stout dagger-like spines (Fig. 68F). Case straight, usually with large
> flat circular pieces of dead leaf attached (Figs 69D–F; note that
> *Potamophylax* larvae often have a similar case), but cylindrical cases
> of butted or overlapping pieces are common, especially when suitable
> leaves become scarce.

> Still and slow-flowing permanent and temporary waters, usually
> among fallen leaves. Widespread and common.

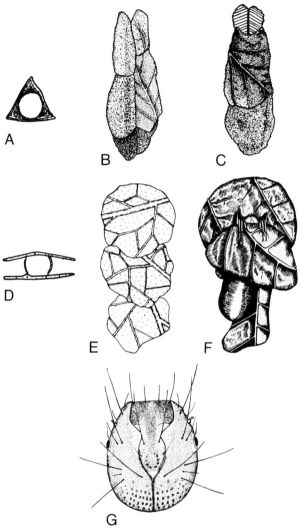

Fig. 69.   **A–C**: case of *Phacopteryx brevipennis*: A, transverse section; B, dorsal view; C, ventral view.   **D–F**: case of *Glyphotaelius pellucidus*: D, transverse section; E, dorsal view; F, ventral view.   **G**: head capsule of *G. pellucidus*.

37(35) Head with a characteristic pattern of dark blotches on a pale
    background (Fig. 70D)—   **Anabolia nervosa** (Curtis)

> Femur of 1st leg frequently with additional setae *fs* on the faces (Fig.
> 68B). Case straight, either of plant pieces arranged longitudinally or
> in a way which produces a chevron pattern in dorsal view (Figs 70A,
> B) or of sand grains, often with one or more long sticks attached
> (Fig. 70C).
>
> Rivers, lakes and ponds; not in temporary waterbodies though larvae
> may be abundant in marginal pools left by falling water levels.
> Widespread and common.

— Pattern of head not as above—   **38**

38 Head with a characteristic dark 'U'-shaped band on a pale back-
    ground; fronto-clypeal band *fb* with parallel longitudinal sides (Fig.
    70E)—   **Nemotaulius punctatolineatus** (Retzius)

> Pleural band absent. Case types similar to those of *Glyphotaelius*
> *pellucidus* (couplet 36) but green leaf pieces may be used.
>
> Larvae recently discovered in pools on blanket bog, Caithness; two
> adult records from Aviemore in the 1960's.

— Pattern of head not as above—   **39**

39 Anterior third of pronotum uniformly darker than posterior two-
    thirds (as in Fig. 70F); (margins and transverse furrow may be even
    darker, Fig. 70G)—   **40**

— Anterior third of pronotum similar in colour to posterior two-thirds
    (Fig. 70H); (margins and transverse furrow may be darker than rest
    of sclerite)—   **44**

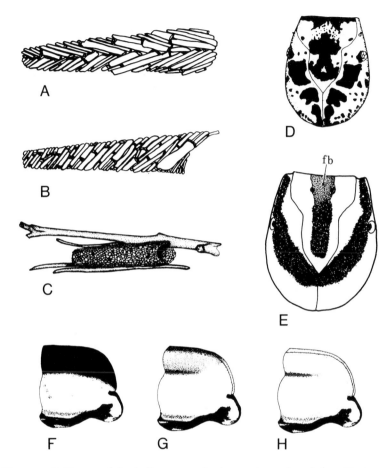

Fig. 70.   **A–C**: case of *Anabolia nervosa*: A, chevron type, dorsal view; B, chevron
type, lateral view; C, sand grain and stick type, ventral view. **D**:
head capsule of *Anabolia nervosa*. **E**: head capsule of *Nemotaulius
punctatolineatus*. **F–H**: pronotum, right half: F, *Limnephilus rhombicus*; G, H, *L. decipiens*.

40 EITHER: proventer (see Fig. 3) with large lateral sternites which are fused with the central prosternite to give a single sclerite which is at least twice as wide as it is high (Figs 71A–D); OR: case of plant pieces arranged tangentially with their ends protruding (Figs 71G–I). (Some larvae have both characters.)—   **41**

> *Limnephilus flavicornis, L. marmoratus,*
> *L. politus* and *L. stigma*
> These are not separable at instar IV:
> head width less than 1·40 mm.

> Case construction often changes during instar V and full-grown larvae may have cases of chunks of plant material (as in Fig. 71J), mollusc shells or mineral particles. The prosternites are always distinctive at instar V but are not always so at instar IV (as shown by Fig. 71E) and sometimes are not apparent then. Head with bands (Fig. 72A).

—   Proventer with small lateral sternites *l* lying a little apart from the central prosternite (Fig. 71F) or with indistinct prosternites AND case of plant pieces arranged longitudinally and often overlapping (e.g. Fig. 75E); occasionally case is triangular in cross-section (Fig. 72D)—   **44**

> Do not continue with the key if the case is missing and the head has distinct bands and a width of less than 1·40 mm; the larva belongs either to the group in part 1 of this couplet or to one of the following species (which sometimes have a dark anterior third to the pronotum): *L. binotatus, L. decipiens, L. nigriceps.*

41 Additional setae present on faces of femora of 3rd legs only; (rarely, there is also 1 seta on femora of 2nd legs)—

> **Limnephilus politus** McLachlan
> Instar V

> Prosternites large and well-pigmented, variable in form (as in Figs 71C, D).

> Lakes and canals. England, Wales and southern Scotland; only common in southern England.

—   Additional setae present on faces of femora of 2nd and 3rd legs—

42

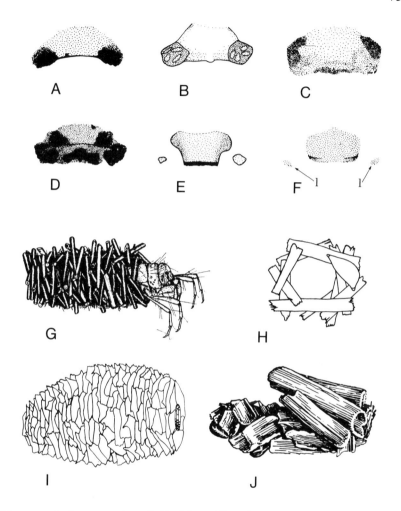

Fig. 71. **A–F**: prosternites: A, B, *Limnephilus stigma*; C, *L. marmoratus;* D, *L. flavicornis*; E, *L. flavicornis*, instar IV; F, *L. incisus*. **G**: larva and case of *L. flavicornis*. **H**: transverse section of case of *L. flavicornis*. **I**: case of *L. stigma*. **J**: case of *L. rhombicus*.

42 Proximal section of trochanter of 3rd leg with 2 or more additional
    setae *as* (Fig. 72B); additional setae are usually also present at a
    similar position on 2nd leg. Lateral prosternites merge in colour with
    central prosternite, which usually has patches of very dark pigment
    (Figs 71C, D)—   **43**

—   Proximal section of trochanters of 2nd and 3rd legs without additional
    setae (Fig. 72C) (or, rarely, with 1 on trochanter of 3rd leg). Lateral
    prosternites prominently dark; central prosternite uniformly pale or
    with any pigmented areas paler than the lateral sternites (Figs 71A,
    B)—   **Limnephilus stigma** Curtis
                                                                      Instar V

    Case characteristically of pieces of grass blade, barrel-shaped (Fig.
    71I). Gills present on 8th abdominal segment.

    Among dense emergent vegetation in marshy areas which may dry
    up in summer. Widespread; common except in south-east England.

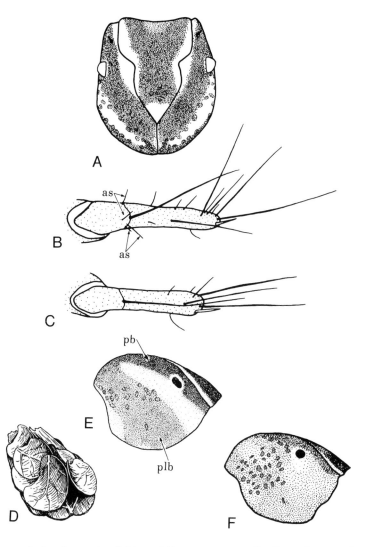

Fig. 72. **A**: head capsule of *Limnephilus marmoratus*. **B, C**: trochanter of 3rd leg, ventral view: B, *L. flavicornis*; C, *L. stigma*. **D**: triangular case of *L. nigriceps*. **E, F**: head capsule, lateral view: E, *L. nigriceps*; F, *L. affinis*.

43   Gill(s) present on 8th abdominal segment*—
                    Limnephilus flavicornis (Fabricius)
                                      Instar V

> A wide variety of still and slow-flowing waters, often among vegetation. Widespread and common.

—   No gills on 8th abdominal segment*—
                    Limnephilus marmoratus Curtis
                                      Instar V

> A wide variety of still and slow-flowing waters, often among vegetation. Widespread and common.

> * This character proved to be reliable for larvae collected at instar V and reared to the adult. It failed for a small proportion of each species when larvae were reared from the egg.

44(39,40) Pleural band *plb* long and distinct, joining parietal band *pb* along coronal suture (Figs 72E, 81C and as in Figs 81F, G)—   **45**

> 1st abdominal venter with 1–3 setae in each anterior group *a* (as in Fig. 76B). Anterior third of pronotum is often much darker than posterior two-thirds (Fig. 70G).

—   Pleural band absent or very indistinct, not joining parietal band along coronal suture; (lateral region of head is uniformly coloured or has brownish patches on a paler background, Fig. 72F)—   **46**

45 Up to 2 additional setae on each face of femora of 2nd and 3rd legs; the total count for all eight faces is only 1–4—
Limnephilus decipiens (Kolenati) (some)

Case similar to that of *L. nigriceps*.

Lakes, canals and dykes with some vegetation. South-east and midland England north to Cheshire and Lincolnshire; locally common. Also in central Ireland.

— Up to 7 additional setae on each face of femora of 2nd and 3rd legs; the total count for all eight faces is 7 or more—
Limnephilus nigriceps (Zetterstedt)

Case straight, of butted or overlapped plant pieces, sometimes triangular in cross-section (Fig. 72D).

Lakes with emergent marginal vegetation. Central Ireland, Scotland and northern England south to Cheshire and Leicestershire; locally common.

46(44) Additional setae *fs* on femora of 2nd and 3rd legs confined to proximal region of anterior faces (Fig. 73A); (*fs* absent from posterior faces)—
Limnephilus fuscicornis (Rambur)

Head predominantly pale (Fig. 73C), sometimes lightly banded. Case curved, of sand grains and/or plant material (Fig. 73B).

Rivers and streams; among boulders on gravelly sand substrata. England, Wales and lowland Scotland; local.

— Additional setae on femora of 2nd and 3rd legs not confined to proximal region of anterior faces—
47

47 Case triangular in cross-section, straight (Figs 69A–C). Femur of 1st leg with additional setae *fs* on anterior and/or posterior faces (as in Fig. 68B)—
Phacopteryx brevipennis (Curtis) (some)

See couplet 36.

— Case circular in cross-section, straight or curved. Femur of 1st leg without additional setae on the faces (as in Fig. 68A)—
48

48 * Metadorsum (Fig. 73D) with setae *is* on soft cuticle between posterior sclerites *p*; anterior-median sclerites *a* pale and ill-defined.
Proximal section of trochanter of 2nd or 3rd leg with 1 or more
additional setae *as* (as in Fig. 77A)—   **49**

— Metadorsum (Fig. 73E) with no setae on soft cuticle between posterior
sclerites *p*; anterior-median sclerites *a* dark and clearly defined.
Proximal section of trochanters of 2nd and 3rd legs with no additional
setae (as in Fig. 77B)—   **50**

* **Limnephilus tauricus** Schmid will arrive here. Information on the larva
comes from the exuviae of a single instar V specimen which was collected by
P. D. Hiley among *L. incisus* in a *Phragmites* bed at Woolhampton, Berkshire.
The larva had additional setae on the proximal section of the trochanters of
the 2nd and 3rd legs and 12 and 16 setae in the anterior-median area *am* on
each side of the mesonotum (see Fig. 74C). There is no useful data on the
metadorsum. Head dark red-brown, without bands (similar to Fig. 80D).
Case straight, of overlapped pieces of plant material (similar to Fig. 84F).
The Woolhampton record is the only recent one; there are old records of
adults from fens in southern and eastern England.

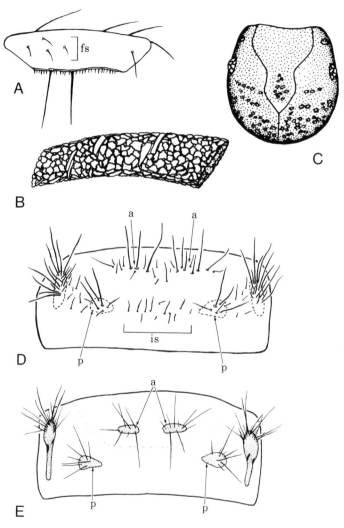

Fig. 73. **A–C**: *Limnephilus fuscicornis*: A, femur of 2nd leg, anterior view; B, case; C, head capsule. **D, E**: metadorsum: D, *L. extricatus*; E, *L. griseus*.

49 Lobe of anal proleg with setae *ls* on soft cuticle by anal slit (Fig. 74A). Mesonotum with 33–70 setae in each anterior–median area at instar V (head width more than 1·05 mm) and 22–37 at instar IV—
Limnephilus hirsutus (Pictet)

> Femora of 2nd and 3rd legs with all ventral edge setae dark in colour. Head variable in colour but without distinct bands. Case curved, of sand grains.

> Permanent hardwater trickles and small streams in open situations: usually clay substratum. Widespread.

— Lobe of anal proleg with no setae on soft cuticle by anal slit (Fig. 74B). Mesonotum with 9–31 setae in each anterior-median area *am* at instar V (head width more than 1·05 mm, Fig. 74C) and 6–14 at instar IV—   **Limnephilus extricatus** McLachlan

> Femora of 2nd and 3rd legs with ventral edge setae usually contrasting in colour (as in Figs 77E, F). Head variable in colour but without distinct bands. Case curved, usually of sand grains (Fig. 74D), sometimes with plant fragments, occasionally entirely of plant material.

> Silty and well-vegetated regions of small rivers, streams, canals and occasionally lakes. Throughout Britain; common.

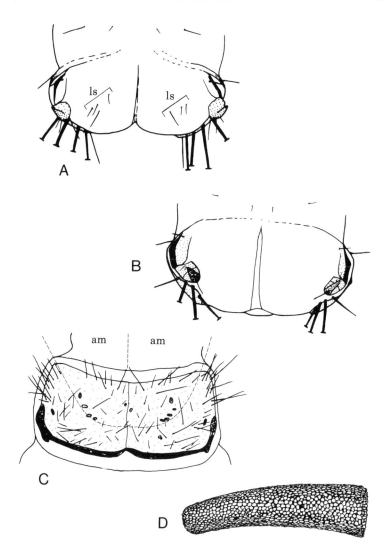

Fig. 74. **A, B**: 9th abdominal segment, posterior view: A, *Limnephilus hirsutus*; B, *L. extricatus*. **C**: mesonotum of *L. extricatus*. **D**: case of *L. extricatus*.

50(48) Case curved (Fig. 75A). Each side of 9th abdominal dorsal sclerite with at least one seta between innermost primary seta I and outermost primary seta O which is more than half as long as seta O (Fig. 75F) AND anterior face of femur of 2nd leg with no additional setae (or, very rarely, with 1)—   **Limnephilus griseus** (L.)

> Head without bands, though posterior tip of fronto-clypeal apotome is often pale and there may be a pale area on posterior region of each parietal (Fig. 75B). Femora with additional face setae usually confined to posterior face of femur of 3rd leg. 1st abdominal venter with a total of 13 or more setae in the anterior groups a, both groups included (as in Fig. 76A). Case of plant material or partly (Fig. 75A) or entirely of sand grains.
>
> Small, often temporary acidic pools in open situations. Widespread; common in upland areas.

— Case straight (Figs 75C, E) or slightly curved (Fig. 75D). EITHER: each side of 9th abdominal dorsal sclerite with all setae between innermost primary seta I and outermost primary seta O less than half as long seta O (Fig. 75G); OR: anterior face of femur of 2nd leg with 1–7 additional setae—   **51**

51 Head width more than 1·00 mm—   **52**

—   Head width less than 1·00 mm—   **53**

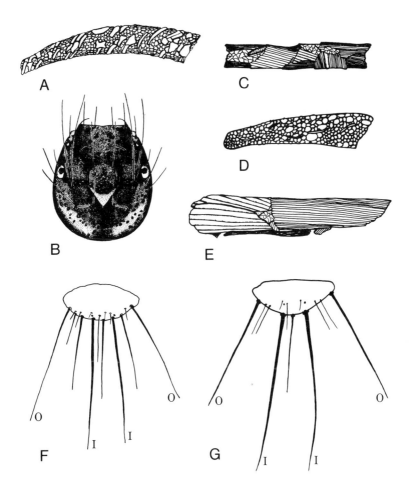

Fig. 75. **A, B**: *Limnephilus griseus:* A, case; B, head capsule. **C–E**: case: C, *L. incisus*; D, *L. affinis*, curved type; E, *L. binotatus*. **F, G**: 9th abdominal dorsal sclerite: F, *L. griseus*; G, *L. binotatus*.

52   Anterior face of femur of 2nd leg with 1–7 additional setae; combined
     count of additional setae on anterior faces of both 2nd legs is 3 or
     more. 1st abdominal venter with anterior setal groups *a* large and
     often merged together (Fig. 76A); total number of setae, both groups
     included, is 10–44 (but, exceptionally, as few as 6)—

                                                Limnephilus affinis Curtis
                                                Limnephilus incisus Curtis
                                                                   Instar V

> Head variable in ground colour but parietal bands are usually visible
> (as in Figs 80A, C). No gills on 8th abdominal segment. Distal
> section of trochanter of 2nd leg, in anterior view, with no dark
> proximo-dorsal setae between the two pale primary setae *ps* (as in
> Fig. 80G). Case of both species is of butted and overlapped pieces of
> plant material, straight (Fig. 75C); that of *L. affinis* may incorporate
> sand grains and small debris (as in Fig. 80H), especially if the
> substratum is devoid of large plant fragments (sand grain cases may
> show slight curvature, Fig. 75D).

> *L. incisus* is found in the tussocky margins of pools, lakes and slow-
> flowing ditches which contract or dry out in summer. *L. affinis* is
> found in similar habitats and also in brackish water. Both species are
> widespread and common.

—   Anterior face of femur of 2nd leg with 0–1 additional setae; combined
     count of additional setae on anterior faces of both 2nd legs is 0–1. 1st
     abdominal venter with anterior setal groups *a* small and distinct
     (Fig. 76B); total number of setae, both groups included, is 2–8 (but
     exceptionally up to 14)—   **Limnephilus binotatus** Curtis
                                                            Instars IV and V

> Head brown, with pale areas around edges of fronto-clypeal apotome
> which may (Fig. 76C) be extensive, or with distinct fronto-clypeal
> and parietal bands. Gills may be present on 8th abdominal segment.
> Distal section of trochanter of each 2nd leg, in anterior view, with 1
> or more dark proximo-dorsal setae *as* between the two pale primary
> setae *ps* (as in Fig. 80E) at instar V and sometimes at instar IV. Case
> straight, of butted and overlapped plant material (Fig. 75E).

> Among emergent vegetation in fens and lake margins in regions which
> lack standing water in summer. Widespread but local.

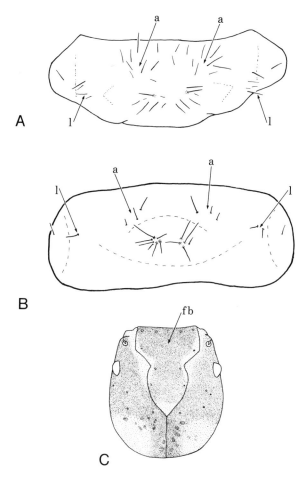

Fig. 76. **A, B**: 1st abdominal segment, ventral view: A, *Limnephilus affinis*; B, *L. binotatus*. **C**: head capsule of *L. binotatus*.

53(51) 1st abdominal venter with 5 or more setae in anterior setal groups *a*, both groups included (see Fig. 76A). Anterior face of femur of 2nd leg with 0–3 additional setae; (the setae are small and pale)—

Limnephilus affinis Curtis
Limnephilus incisus Curtis
Instar IV

> See inset section of the first part of couplet 52.

— 1st abdominal venter with 2–4 setae in anterior setal groups *a*, both groups included (see Fig. 76B). Anterior face of femur of 2nd leg with no additional setae—   **Limnephilus binotatus** Curtis
Instar IV (a few)

> See inset section of the second part of couplet 52.

54(31) Proximal section of trochanter of 2nd or 3rd leg with 1 or more additional setae *as* (Fig. 77A)—   **Limnephilus coenosus** Curtis

> Head dark brown, without pale areas. Case curved or straight, of small pieces of plant material (Fig. 77C).
>
> Small, usually permanent, shallow pools on heather moors and raised bogs. Scotland, Wales and England south to Staffordshire; also Somerset and western Ireland. Common in upland areas.

— Proximal section of trochanters of 2nd and 3rd legs with no additional setae (Fig. 77B)—   **55**

55 Case curved (Figs 77D, 78E, 79B, D). Femora of 2nd and/or 3rd legs with ventral edge setae *vs* contrasting in colour (Figs 77E, F)—   **56**

— Case straight (Figs 80H, 81H, 83H, 84F). Femora of 2nd and 3rd legs with all ventral edge setae *vs* dark in colour (Figs 84A, B; except in the very rare species *Grammotaulius nitidus*)—   **61**

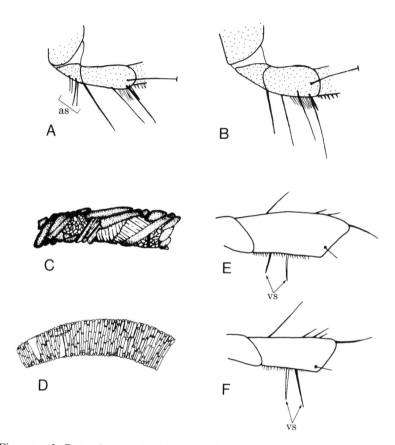

Fig. 77. **A, B**: trochanter of 3rd leg, posterior view: A, *Limnephilus coenosus*; B, *L. bipunctatus*. **C**: case of *L. coenosus*. **D**: case of *L. sparsus*. **E, F**: femur of *L. sparsus*, posterior view: E, 2nd leg; F, 3rd leg.

56 Metadorsum with a row of setae *is* on soft cuticle between posterior sclerites *p* (as in Fig. 73D; there may be as few as 3 setae in the row)— **Limnephilus sparsus** Curtis

> Head red-brown. Case either of small plant pieces arranged tangentially (Fig. 77D) or of sand grains.
>
> Temporary pools, sometimes as small as hoof-prints in marshy ground, usually with overhanging grass or rushes. Widespread and common.

— Metadorsum with no row of setae on soft cuticle between posterior sclerites (as in Fig. 73E)— 57

57 Lateral sclerite of anal proleg with several squat, yellow or brown, setae *ss* on the face (Fig. 78A); (the squat setae are easily detached when adherent debris is removed, but their broad alveoli will be clearly visible)— **Rhadicoleptus alpestris** (Kolenati)

> All sclerites pale golden brown with little darker pigmentation. Case of small plant pieces arranged tangentially (as in Fig. 77D).
>
> Small, temporary, shallow peat pools amongst tussocks of vegetation, especially *Eriophorum vaginatum* L.; upland watershed bogs and lowland raised bogs. Wales and northern England, also Dumfries & Galloway and Speyside.

— Lateral sclerite of anal proleg with no squat setae on the face (Fig. 78B)— 58

58 Lobe of anal proleg with setae *ls* on soft cuticle by anal slit (as in Fig. 74A). 9th abdominal dorsal sclerite with all setae, other than innermost primary setae *I*, less than half as long as outermost primary setae *O* (Fig. 78C)— **Limnephilus vittatus** (Fabricius)

> Central prosternite about twice as wide as it is high (Fig. 78D). Dorsal surface of head usually very dark brown, normally evenly coloured but posterior tip of fronto-clypeal apotome may be pale. Case of sand grains (Fig. 78E), anterior end typically notched in dorsal view (Fig. 78F).
>
> Sandy or silty areas of lakes, ponds and temporary pools. Widespread and common.

— Lobe of anal proleg with no setae on soft cuticle by anal slit (as in Fig. 74B). 9th abdominal dorsal sclerite with at least one seta, other than innermost primary setae *I*, which is more than half as long as outermost primary setae *O* (as in Figs 75F, G)— 59

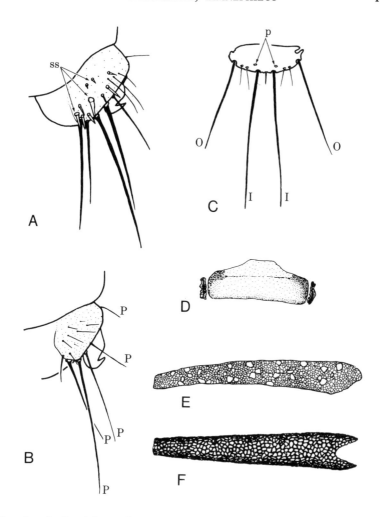

Fig. 78. **A, B**: right anal proleg, dorsal view: A, *Rhadicoleptus alpestris*; B, *Limnephilus centralis*.   **C–F**: *L. vittatus*: C, 9th abdominal dorsal sclerite; D, prosternites; E, case, lateral view; F, case, dorsal view.

59   Central prosternite about twice as wide as it is high (Fig. 79A)—
                          Limnephilus centralis Curtis
                              Instars IV (some) and V

At instar V (head width 0·90–1·30 mm), 1st abdominal venter with
1–11 setae in each lateral setal group *l* (as in Fig. 76A) and lateral
sclerite of anal proleg with 11–18 setae (including the 5 primary setae
P along posterior edge, Fig. 78B). Head brown, usually with pale
posterior tip to fronto-clypeal apotome. Case of sand grains (Fig.
79B) or, occasionally, of small pieces of plant material.

Temporary pools and runnels on moorland; also in marshes, ditches
and ponds. Widespread and common.

—   Central prosternite about one-and-a-half times as wide as it is high
     (Fig. 79C) or not apparent—   **60**

60   Head width more than 0·90 mm— **Limnephilus bipunctatus** Curtis

Head width at instar V more than 1·30 mm. At instar IV (head width
1·00–1·20 mm), 1st abdominal venter with 1–3 setae in each lateral
group *l* (see Fig. 76A) and lateral sclerite of anal proleg with 8–11
setae (including the 5 primary setae *P* along posterior edge, see Fig.
78B). Head brown with a pale posterior tip to fronto-clypeal apotome
and a pale area on posterior region of each parietal (as in Fig. 75B).
Case of small mineral particles, often embellished with fragments of
decaying grass blades or roots (Fig. 79D), or partly or entirely of
small pieces of plant material.

Streams, ditches and pools which may dry up in summer. Throughout
Britain; local.

—   Head width less than 0·90 mm—   **Limnephilus centralis** Curtis
                                               Instar IV (some)

See inset section of the first part of couplet 59.

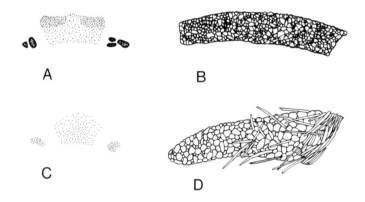

Fig. 79. **A, B**: *Limnephilus centralis:* A, prosternites; B, case. **C, D**: *L. bipunctatus:* C, prosternites; D, case.

61(55) Anterior-lateral gills present on 2nd abdominal segment (see Fig. 4C)— **63**

—   No anterior-lateral gills on 2nd abdominal segment—   **62**

62   Head with pale areas around edges of fronto-clypeal apotome (Figs 80A–C) and usually with distinct fronto-clypeal *fb* and parietal *pb* bands (Figs 80A, B). Distal section of trochanter of 2nd or 3rd leg, in anterior view, with 1 or more dark proximo-dorsal setae *as* between the two pale primary setae *ps* (Fig. 80E) or with additional setae *ds* arising dorsal to the suture (Fig. 80F)— **Limnephilus lunatus** Curtis

> 1st abdominal venter with some setae in posterior *p* and lateral *l* setal groups arising from small pigmented areas (as in Fig. 82A), most conspicuous at instar IV. Case variously constructed, of plant material, mineral particles or a mixture (Fig. 80H); (if case is of plant pieces arranged tangentially, or the prosternite is wider than it is high, see *L. rhombicus* via the first part of couplet 64).

> Among aquatic vegetation in all types of permanent waterbody, but not in fast-flowing water. Widespread and common.

—   Head dark brown with no pale areas around edges of fronto-clypeal apotome, though posterior tip of apotome may be pale (Fig. 80D). Distal section of trochanters of 2nd and 3rd legs, in anterior view, with no dark proximo-dorsal setae between the two pale primary setae *ps* and with no additional setae arising dorsal to the suture (Fig. 80G)— **Limnephilus auricula** Curtis

> 1st abdominal venter with no setae arising from a pigmented area. Metadorsum with anterior-median sclerites small, dark and clearly defined (if not, see *L. luridus*, couplet 74). Case of butted and overlapped plant pieces (as in Fig. 75C).

> Temporary grassy pools and ditches. Widespread and common.

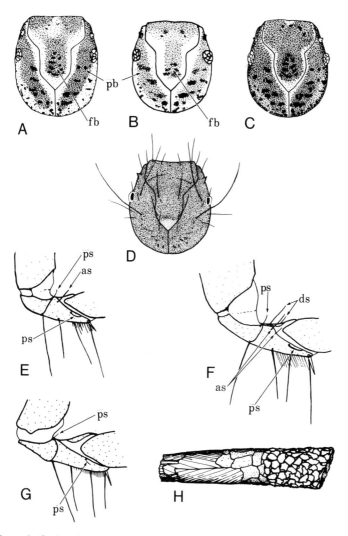

Fig. 80. **A–C**: head capsule of *Limnephilus lunatus*. **D**: head capsule of *L. auricula*. **E–G**: trochanter of 2nd leg, anterior view: E, *L. lunatus*, instar IV; F, *L. lunatus*, instar V; G, *L. auricula*. **H**: case of *L. lunatus*.

63(61) Head with fronto-clypeal *fb* and parietal *pb* bands comprising more or less uniform areas of dark colour, the pale ground colour being visible between the bands for most of their length (Figs 81C, D)—   **64**

—   Head without obvious fronto-clypeal and parietal bands, though there may be small pale areas around edges of fronto-clypeal apotome (Fig. 84E)—   **70**

64   EITHER: proventer (see Fig. 3) with large lateral sternites which are fused with the central prosternite to give a single sclerite which is at least twice as wide as it is high (as in Figs 71A–D) or lie very close to the central prosternite (Fig. 81A); OR: case of plant pieces arranged tangentially with their ends protruding (as in Figs 71G, H); (some larvae have both characters)—   **65**

          Case construction often changes during instar V and full-grown larvae may have cases made of chunks of plant material (Fig. 71J), mollusc shells or mineral particles. The prosternites are always distinctive at instar V (head width more than 1·50 mm) but are not always so at instar IV (as in Fig. 71E) and sometimes are not apparent. Anterior third of pronotum always uniformly darker than posterior two-thirds (Fig. 70F).

—   Proventer with small lateral sternites *l* lying a little apart from the central prosternite (Fig. 81B) or with indistinct prosternites AND case of plant pieces arranged longitudinally and often overlapping (Fig. 75E); occasionally case is triangular in cross-section (as in Fig. 72D)—   **66**

          Do not continue with the key if the case is missing, the anterior third of the pronotum is uniformly darker than the posterior two-thirds and the head width is less than 1·50 mm; the larva belongs to one of the following species: *L. rhombicus*, *L. politus*, *L. binotatus*, *L. decipiens*.

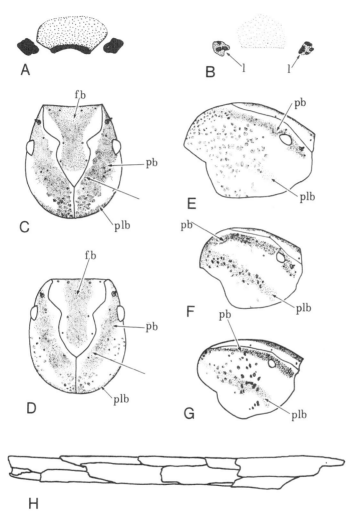

Fig. 81. **A–B**: prosternites: A, *Limnephilus rhombicus*; B, *L. decipiens*. **C, D**: head capsule: C, *L. decipiens*; D, *L. fuscinervis*. **E–G**: head capsule, lateral view: E, *L. borealis*; F, *L. subcentralis*; G, *L. fuscinervis*. **H**: case of *L. fuscinervis*.

65   Head width more than 1·50 mm—   **Limnephilus rhombicus** (L.)
                                                              Instar V

A wide variety of still and slow-flowing waters. Widespread and common.

NOTE: A few *L. politus* (see couplet 41) appear here. Instar V larvae of *L. rhombicus* are found in winter and spring while those of *L. politus* are found during summer.

—   Head width less than 1·50 mm—   **Limnephilus rhombicus** (L.)
                                                             Instar IV
                                          Limnephilus politus (McLachlan)
                                                              (some)

66(64) Pleural band *plb* long and distinct, joining parietal band *pb* along coronal suture (Figs 81C, D, F)—   **68**

—   Pleural band absent, indistinct or short and not joining parietal band along coronal suture (Fig. 81E and as in Fig. 72F)—   **67**

67 Lateral surface of head predominantly pale with strongly contrasting muscle attachment spots (Fig. 81E). Posterior region of parietal band lies well clear of fronto-clypeal suture (as in Fig. 81D, region arrowed)
Limnephilus borealis (Zetterstedt)

Anterior edge of fronto-clypeal band *fb* narrow (as in Fig. 81D) or broad (as in Fig. 81C). Case long and slender, of overlapping pieces of plant material (as in Fig. 81H). Found during summer.

Lakes and pools; amongst plants or litter of *Carex* and *Phragmites*. Highland Scotland; locally common.

— Lateral surface of head predominantly brown, without strongly contrasting muscle attachment spots (as in Fig. 72F). Posterior region of parietal band touches fronto-clypeal suture (as in Fig. 81C)—
Limnephilus binotatus Curtis

Anterior edge of fronto-clypeal band *fb* always broad (as in Fig. 81C). Found from autumn to spring. See couplet 52 for case, habitat and distribution.

68(66) Posterior region of parietal band *pb* approaches or touches fronto-clypeal suture and slopes away again (arrow, Fig. 81C)—
Limnephilus decipiens (Kolenati)

Anterior edge of fronto-clypeal band *fb* always broad (Fig. 81C). Femur of 1st leg with both ventral edge setae *vs* pale in colour (as in Fig. 68B). Case of butted or overlapped plant pieces, sometimes triangular in cross-section (as in Fig. 72D).

Lakes, canals and dykes with some vegetation. South-east and midland England north to Cheshire and Lincolnshire; locally common. Also in central Ireland.

— Posterior region of parietal band *pb* lies well clear of fronto-clypeal suture and runs more or less parallel to it (arrow, Fig. 81D)—   **69**

69 Muscle attachment spots between parietal band *pb* and pleural band *plb* are as dark as those in the bands (Fig. 81G)—
Limnephilus fuscinervis (Zetterstedt)

Anterior edge of fronto-clypeal band *fb* narrow (Fig. 81D) or broad (as in Fig. 81C). Femur of 1st leg with ventral edge setae *vs* contrasting in colour (as in Fig. 68A). Case long and slender, of overlapping pieces of plant material (Fig. 81H).

Lakes and pools; amongst plants or litter of *Carex* and *Phragmites*. Central Ireland; locally common.

— Muscle attachment spots between parietal band *pb* and pleural band *plb* are absent or very much paler than those in the bands (Fig. 81F)—
Limnephilus subcentralis Brauer

Anterior edge of fronto-clypeal band *fb* narrow (as in Fig. 81D). Femur of 1st leg with ventral edge setae *vs* similar or contrasting in colour (as in Figs. 68A, B). Case long and slender, of overlapping pieces of plant material (as in Fig. 81H).

Lakes and pools with emergent marginal vegetation. Southern and central highlands of Scotland.

70(63)Head width more than 2·10 mm—
           Genus GRAMMOTAULIUS, instar V, **77**

—   Head width less than 2·10 mm—   **71**

71   Head width more than 1·20 mm—   **72**

—   Head width less than 1·20 mm—   **73**

72   1st abdominal venter with 13–36 setae in anterior setal groups a, both groups included (Fig. 82A). Mesonotum with 8–21 setae in each anterior-median area am (see Fig. 74C)—   (instar V), **74**

> Distal section of trochanters of 2nd and 3rd legs, in anterior view, with no dark proximo-dorsal setae between the two pale primary setae ps and with no additional setae arising dorsal to the suture (as in Fig. 80G).

—   1st abdominal venter with 2–12 (exceptionally up to 14) setae in anterior setal groups a, both groups included. Mesonotum with 1–8 setae in each anterior-median area—   **75**

> Distal section of trochanter of 2nd or 3rd leg, in anterior view, frequently with 1 or more dark proximo-dorsal setae as between the two pale primary setae ps or with additional setae ds arising dorsal to the suture (as in Figs 80E, F). Each side of 9th abdominal dorsal sclerite with all setae between innermost primary seta I and outermost primary seta O less than half as long as seta O (Fig. 75G).

73(71) 1st abdominal venter with 5–18 setae in anterior setal groups *a*, both groups included (see Fig. 82A). Mesonotum with 3–10 setae in each anterior-median area *am* (see Fig. 74C)—   (instar IV), **74**

> Distal section of trochanters of 2nd and 3rd legs, in anterior view, with no dark proximo-dorsal setae between the two pale primary setae *ps* (as in Fig. 80G).

— 1st abdominal venter with 2–4 setae in anterior setal groups *a*, both groups included. Mesonotum with 1–3 setae in each anterior-median area—   **75**

> Distal section of trochanter of 2nd or 3rd leg frequently with 1 or more dark proximo-dorsal setae *as* between the two pale primary setae *ps* (as in Fig. 80E). Each side of 9th abdominal dorsal sclerite with all setae between innermost primary seta *I* and outermost primary seta *O* less than half as long as seta *O* (as in Fig. 82D).

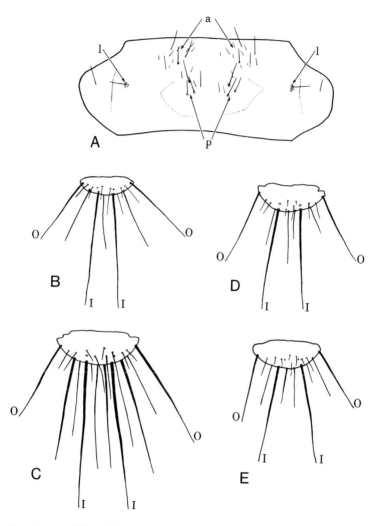

Fig. 82.   **A**: 1st abdominal segment, ventral view, of *Limnephilus ignavus*.   **B,**
C: 9th abdominal dorsal sclerite of *L. luridus*: B, instar IV; C, instar
V.   **D, E**: 9th abdominal dorsal sclerite of *L. ignavus*.

74(72,73) Each side of 9th abdominal dorsal sclerite with at least one seta between innermost primary seta I and outermost primary seta O which is three-quarters or more of the length of seta O at instar IV (Fig. 82B) and equal to seta O at instar V (Fig. 82C). Lateral sclerite of anal proleg with one seta (arrow, Figs 83A, B) next to innermost seta iP of the five primary setae P which is more than half as long as seta iP (Figs 83A, B). Metadorsum with anterior-median sclerites a ill-defined (Fig. 83D) and paler than the mesonotum—

Limnephilus luridus Curtis

>Head reddish brown with slightly paler muscle attachment spots (Fig. 83F). Case of butted and overlapped pieces of plant material, smooth and slightly barrel-shaped when full-sized (Fig. 83H).
>
>Acidic, usually temporary, pools with much dead plant material. Widespread and common.

— Each side of 9th abdominal dorsal sclerite with all setae between innermost primary seta I and outermost primary seta O less than half as long as seta O at instar IV and no more than three-quarters as long as seta O at instar V (Figs 82D, E). Lateral sclerite of anal proleg with all setae next to innermost seta iP of the five primary setae P less than half as long as seta iP (Fig. 83C). Metadorsum with anterior-median sclerites a small, clearly defined (Fig. 83E) and as dark as the mesonotum—   **Limnephilus ignavus** McLachlan

>Head dark brown with even darker muscle attachment spots (Fig. 83G). 1st abdominal venter with some setae in posterior p and lateral l setal groups arising from small pigmented areas (Fig. 82A; if not, see *L. auricula*, couplet 62). Case of butted and overlapped pieces of plant material (as in Fig. 75C).
>
>Shallow pools and marshes with flowing water. Widespread but local; most frequent in Scotland.

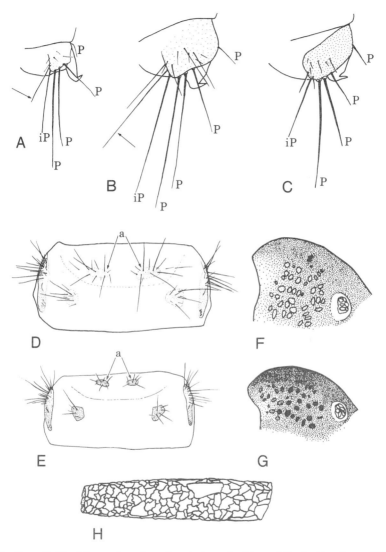

Fig. 83. **A–C**: right anal proleg, dorsal view: A, *Limnephilus luridus*, instar IV;
B, *L. luridus*, instar V; C, *L. ignavus*. **D, E**: metadorsum: D, *L.
luridus*; E, *L. ignavus*. **F, G**: part of right side of head capsule, lateral
view: F, *L. luridus*; G, *L. ignavus*. **H**: case of *L. luridus*.

75(72, 73) Gill(s) present on 8th abdominal segment—   **76**

—   No gills on 8th abdominal segment—   **78**

76   Head width more than 1·30 mm—
                    Genus GRAMMOTAULIUS, instar IV, **77**

—   Head width less than 1·30 mm—   **Limnephilus binotatus** Curtis
                                                        Instar IV (some)
        See the second part of couplet 52.

77(70,76) Femora of 2nd and 3rd legs with all ventral edge setae *vs*
        dark in colour and similar in size (Figs 84A, B)—
                    Grammotaulius nigropunctatus (Retzius)

        Head brown, often with small pale areas around edges of fronto-
        clypeal apotome (Fig. 84E). At instar IV, 9th abdominal dorsal
        sclerite has 8–9 setae, as in Fig. 78C (if there are 10–16, see *L.
        binotatus*, couplet 52). Distal region of trochanters of 2nd and 3rd
        legs with a ventral row of long flexuous spines *lp* (as in Fig. 84G; if
        not, see *L. elegans*, couplet 78). Gills almost always present at 2 or
        more sites on 8th abdominal segment. Case of overlapped pieces of
        plant material (Fig. 84F), often much longer than the larva.

        Amongst emergent vegetation in pools and ditches which may dry
        up during summer. Widespread and common.

—   Femora of 2nd and 3rd legs with ventral edge setae *vs* contrasting in
        colour and size (Figs 84C, D)—   **Grammotaulius nitidus** (Müller)

        (Based on a description by Lepneva 1971).

        Head pattern and case similar to those of *G. nigropunctatus*.

        No larvae are known from Britain or Ireland; in the Soviet Union
        they have been found in small overgrown waterbodies, especially
        swampy pools which dry up in summer. There are post–1950 adult
        records from the Norfolk and Suffolk Broads and the Somerset
        Levels, and older records from the Cambridgeshire Fens and Deal
        in Kent.

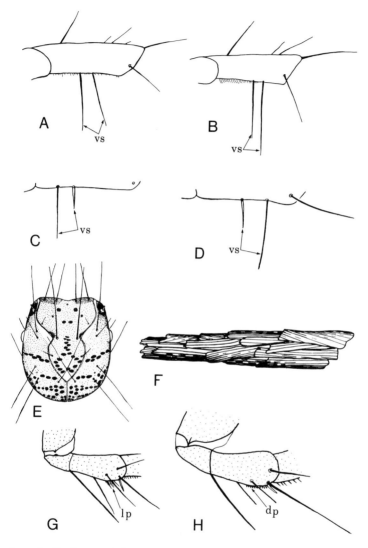

Fig. 84. **A, B**: femur of *Grammotaulius nigropunctatus*, posterior view: A, 2nd leg; B, 3rd leg. **C, D**: ventral edge of femur of *G. nitidus*, posterior view: C, 2nd leg; D, 3rd leg. **E**: head capsule of *G. nigropunctatus*. **F**: case of *G. nigropunctatus*. **G, H**: trochanter of 3rd leg, posterior view: G, *Limnephilus binotatus*, instar IV; H, *L. elegans*.

78(75) Head with pale areas around edges of fronto-clypeal apotome
(Fig. 76C)—   **Limnephilus binotatus** Curtis
(some)

> Distal region of trochanters of 2nd and, usually, 3rd legs with a
> ventral row of long flexuous spines lp (Fig. 84G). See the second
> part of couplet 52.

—   Head without pale areas around edges of fronto-clypeal apotome,
though posterior tip of apotome may be pale (as in Fig. 80D)—
Limnephilus elegans (Curtis)

> Distal region of trochanters of 2nd and 3rd legs with a ventral row
> of short dagger-like spines dp and no long flexuous spines (Fig. 84H;
> if not, see *L. borealis*, couplet 67). Head brown. Case usually of
> overlapped pieces of plant material (as in Fig. 84F) at instar V, but
> at instar IV it may be made of cut pieces of root arranged in a spiral.

> Small pools on raised bogs and in acid fens. Widespread but local.

Family MOLANNIDAE

Both British species (Table 9) live in still or slow-flowing water on a substratum of sand or fine gravel. They have distinctive cases of sand grains cemented together to form a convex shield-shaped plate incorporating a central tube (Figs 85F–H). The wings of the plate extend forwards as a hood covering the anterior opening of the tube (Fig. 85F); (the lateral wings are easily damaged and may be accidentally broken off during sampling and sorting). The cases are very well camouflaged against the bare substrata on which the larvae often live. They are only conspicuous when the larvae move, which they do in jerks achieved by bounding leaps.

Molannid larvae are characterized by the presence of numerous spines on the tarsal claw of the third leg. This unique feature is easily seen at the final instar (Figs 85A, C) but at early instars the spines are short (Figs 85B, D) and the slender claw might be mistaken, at low magnification, for a normal claw. Another notable feature is the presence on the tibia of the first leg of an obvious ventral process bearing a single stout seta (Fig. 11E); (a process is also present on the tibia of the second leg). Molannids have moderately long antennae arising close to the anterior margin of the head capsule and may possibly be misidentified as leptocerids (Key to Families, couplet 8). However, the antenna is broad at the base (arrow, Fig. 85E), and even at instar II the length/width ratio does not exceed 4.

M. angustata has a long flight period (May to September) and instars III–V have been found in winter. M. albicans has a short flight period in late summer and overwinters as young larvae (Leader 1968); Mr. R. A. Jenkins has collected instars II and III at the end of April.

TABLE 9. HEAD WIDTHS OF MOLANNIDAE
Ranges (and *n*) of head widths (mm) at instars II to V.

Species	Instar			
	II	III	IV	V
Molanna albicans	0·31 (1)	0·43–0·45 (5)	—	0·90–1·02 (4)
M. angustata	0·30–0·32 (7)	0·41–0·49 (10)	0·57–0·77 (13)	0·90–1·15 (10)

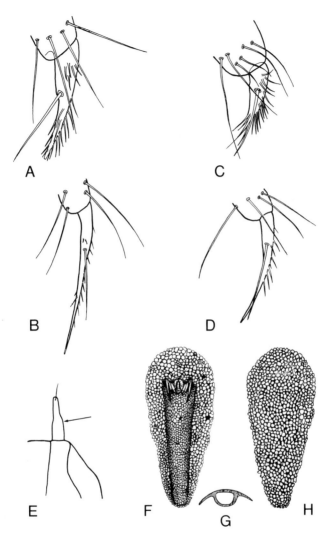

Fig. 85. **A–D**: tarsal claw of 3rd leg, posterior view: A, *Molanna albicans*, instar V; B, *M. albicans*, instar III; C, *M. angustata*, instar V; D, *M. angustata*, instar III. **E**: anterior-lateral region of head capsule of *M. angustata*, instar II. **F–H**: case of *M. angustata*: F, ventral view; G, transverse section; H, dorsal view.

Key to larvae

1   Dorsal surface of anal proleg lateral sclerite with one long, curved, thick seta *ss* (Fig. 86A). Posterior part of fronto-clypeal apotome dark (arrow, Fig. 86C)—   **Molanna albicans** (Zetterstedt)

   Small upland lakes in Wales, lakes in central and northern Scotland, lakes and slow-flowing rivers in central Ireland. Local.

—   Dorsal surface of anal proleg lateral sclerite with several shorter, thick setae *ss* (Fig. 86B). Posterior part of fronto-clypeal apotome pale (arrow, Fig. 86D)—   **Molanna angustata** Curtis

   England north to Cumbria and Yorkshire; often common in lakes, pools, slow-flowing rivers and canals.

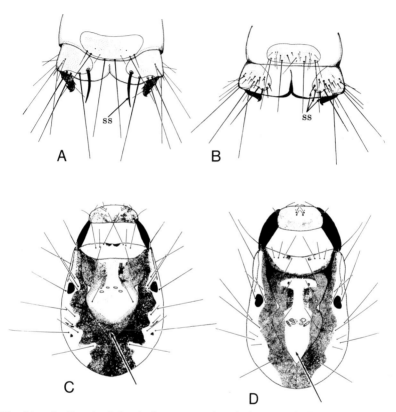

Fig. 86. **A, B**: 9th abdominal segment, dorsal view: A, *Molanna albicans*; B, *M. angustata*. **C**: head of *M. albicans*. **D**: head of *M. angustata*.

Family ODONTOCERIDAE

Odontocerum albicorne (Scopoli) is the only British representative of this family. It is a common species, widespread in stony streams and rivers. The larvae are omnivorous scavengers, most active at night (Elliott 1970).

The case is curved and composed of sand grains (Fig. 87C). Its construction differs from that of other caddis cases, in which building materials are joined together around an internal silken tube. In the *O. albicorne* case, each sand grain is carefully mortared to its neighbours with silk and the joints are reinforced internally with silken braces (Fig. 87F). The resultant case is very strong and rigid, and snaps without first deforming if subjected to bending stress. The posterior end of the case is also distinctive, the opening being protected by a pebble (Fig. 87D). Before pupating the larva also protects the anterior opening of the case with a pebble (Fig. 87E).

The larvae are readily recognizable at instars IV and V by the presence of a distinctive but somewhat variable anchor-shaped mark on the fronto-clypeal apotome (Fig. 14I) and the arrangement of sclerites on the metadorsum (Fig. 87A). At instars II and III the fronto-clypeal mark is absent or indistinct and the posterior metadorsal sclerite is ill-defined (Fig. 87B). These small larvae might be mistaken for sericostomatids but are distinguished by the characteristic anal proleg claw (Fig. 14H) which has a gently curved crook and lacks accessory hooks, and by the presence on the anal proleg of no more than five setae (excluding those on the claw, Figs 14E, F). *Odontocerum albicorne* and *Sericostoma personatum* are often found together under stones.

The life cycle of *O. albicorne* in a small stream in the English Lake District has been studied by Elliott (1982). The species was univoltine, with five larval instars. Consideration of head widths of prepupae, sex of pupae and case lengths revealed two distinct size groups within instar V, smaller and larger groups corresponding to future male and female pupae respectively (Table 10). The larvae overwintered mainly in instars III or V. Instar III larvae grew rapidly in spring to form the 'female' group in instar V. The flight period is between early summer and autumn.

TABLE 10.   HEAD WIDTHS OF ODONTOCERIDAE
Ranges (and *n*) of head widths (mm) at instars II to V of *Odontocerum albicorne*. (After Elliott 1982).

Instar

II	III	IV	V
0·35–0·60 (86)	0·65–0·85 (313)	0·90–1·35 (256)	male 1·40–1·65 (207)
			female 1·70–2·10 (107)

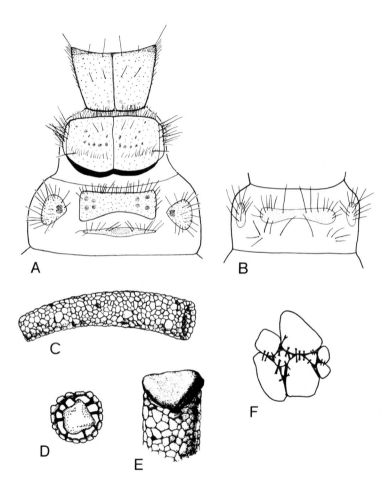

Fig. 87. *Odontocerum albicorne*. **A**: thorax, dorsal view. **B**: metathorax, dorsal view, instar II. **C, D**: case: C, lateral view; D, posterior end. **E**: anterior end of pupal case. **F**: part of interior surface of case showing silken braces.

Family PHRYGANEIDAE

Phryganeid larvae live in tubular cases made from pieces of plant stem or leaves. Some species are very large, reaching 40 mm in length when full-grown. Most have conspicuously banded heads (e.g. Figs 90A, C, E) and spirally whorled cases (Fig. 88B), though the spiral may not be obvious in the early instar case (Fig. 88A). All are readily recognizable by the presence of prominent lateral protuberances on the first abdominal segment, *and* the mesodorsum and metadorsum being largely unsclerotized and resembling each other in setal arrangement (Fig. 7H).

Larvae are encountered in a wide variety of still and slow-flowing waters, such as ponds, lakes, bogs and canals. Most species reach the final instar during spring and early summer. Bray (1966) summarized the distribution of the ten species; the most important additional records given here concern *Trichostegia minor* and *Hagenella clathrata*. Head widths of larvae are given in Table 11.

Larvae of this family often leave their cases when disturbed, in contrast to other tube-cased caddis which are reluctant to do so; they also re-enter them more readily. The full-grown larva of *Agrypnia pagetana* frequently utilizes a piece of hollow stem of reed or horsetail as its case. Some species have the unusual habit of adding length to the case just before pupation; the majority of caddis shorten the case at that time.

The arrangement of the coxal combs (comb-like spines on the coxae, Figs 91A–E) is used at several points in the key. The characters may be difficult to use at first (especially at instar III and with long-preserved larvae in which the comb colour may have faded) but, once mastered, they are invaluable. They are best seen with the coxae inclined at an angle of about 45° to the vertical using a magnification of at least ×50.

TABLE 11.   HEAD WIDTHS OF PHRYGANEIDAE
Ranges of head widths (mm) at instars II to V.

| Species | Instar | | | |
	II	III	IV	V
Agrypnia crassi-cornis	0·59–0·74	0·85–1·15	1·33–1·78	1·96–2·55
A. obsoleta	*0·48–0·59	0·74–0·92	1·04–1·40	1·52–2·08
A. pagetana	0·48–0·55	0·66–0·85	1·00–1·18	1·44–2·02
A. picta	—	—	—	1·45–2·15
A. varia	*0·44–0·55	0·70–0·81	1·04–1·29	1·52–2·04
Hagenella clathrata	0·68	0·86	1·16–1·36	1·76–2·28
Oligotricha striata	0·44–0·55	0·66–0·81	1·07–1·29	1·55–2·07
Phryganea bipunctata	*0·55–0·70	0·85–1·09	1·29–1·66	1·93–2·66
P. grandis	*—	—	—	2·44–2·60
Trichostegia minor	0·40	0·52–0·54	0·84–0·91	1·13–1·44

*Not keyed to species at this instar.

Key to larvae

1   1st abdominal segment with dorsal and lateral protuberances (Fig. 89A)—   **2**

—   1st abdominal segment with only lateral protuberances (Fig. 88C)—
    Trichostegia minor (Curtis)

Fronto-clypeal *fb* and parietal *pb* bands broad, often abutting for much of their length (Fig. 88D); head paler without bands at instar II. Pronotum dark, without conspicuous pale bands. Case of pieces of dead leaves arranged longitudinally but not in a spiral (Fig. 88C).

Woods and fens; found over winter in stagnant leaf-filled pools and ditches which dry up or considerably diminish during summer. England; also a few sites in Wales.

2   Dorsal surface of head and pronotum largely plain brown without conspicuous dark bands (Figs 88E, F). On 1st leg, apical seta of tibia and basal seta of tarsal claw are slightly curved, lie close to the leg and do not arise from a prominence (arrows, Fig. 88G)—
    Hagenella clathrata (Kolenati)

Case slightly curved, of rectangular pieces of dead leaves joined end-to-end in uniform rings.

Shallow water-filled hollows among tussocks of grasses and sedges. Very rare; recent records from two areas of raised bog ('mosses') in the north-west midlands of England and the Welsh borders and from one site near Aviemore.

—   Dorsal surface of head and pronotum yellow or brown with conspicuous dark bands (Figs 89A, B; 90A, C, E). On 1st leg, apical seta of tibia and basal seta of tarsal claw are straight, do not lie close to the leg, and arise from a prominence (arrows, Fig. 88H)—   **3**

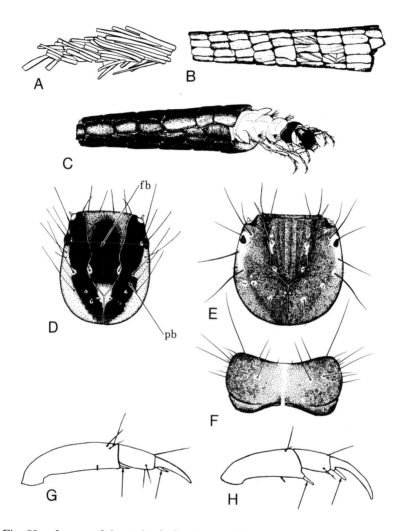

Fig. 88. **A**: case of *Agrypnia obsoleta*, instar III. **B**: case of *Phryganea grandis*, instar V. **C, D**: *Trichostegia minor*: C, larva in case; D, head capsule. **E–G**: *Hagenella clathrata*: E, head capsule; F, pronotum; G, tibia and tarsus of 1st leg, anterior view. **H**: tibia and tarsus of 1st leg, anterior view, of *A. varia*.

3 Parietal bands *pb* almost parallel, continuous posteriorly with longitudinal dark bands on dorsum of thoracic and abdominal segments
   (Fig. 89A); fronto-clypeal band absent—   **Oligotricha striata** (L.)

> Deep pools and ditches, particularly those with acid peaty water.
> Common in Scotland and northern England, rare elsewhere in Bri-
> tain; no recent Irish records.

— Parietal bands *pb* converging towards coronal suture (Figs 89B, 90A,
   C, E), no longitudinal dark bands on dorsum of thoracic or abdominal
   segments; fronto-clypeal band *fb* present (Figs 89B; 90A, C, E)— **4**

4 Parietal bands *pb* short, extending anteriorly only to eyes (Fig. 89B).
   Anal proleg with a gill-like process near its base (arrow, Fig. 89C) at
   instars III–V (head width more than 0·8 mm)—
                           Agrypnia crassicornis (McLachlan)

> Case first built of fragments of *Chara* arranged spirally; later, pieces
> of leaf are used and the spiral pattern is less obvious.

> Known only from Malham Tarn, Yorkshire.

— Parietal bands *pb* long, extending anteriorly to bases of mandibles
   (Figs 90A, C, E). Anal proleg without a gill-like process near its
   base—   **5**

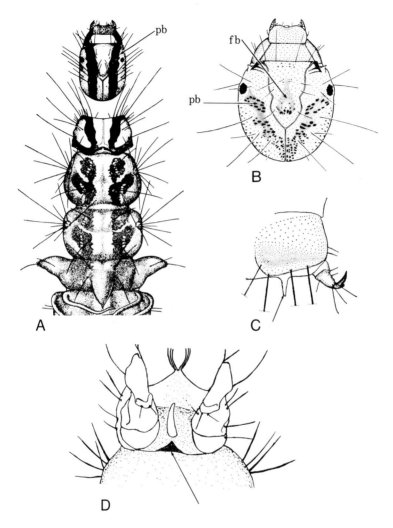

Fig. 89.   **A**: head, thorax and 1st abdominal segment, dorsal view, of *Oligotricha striata*.   **B, C**: *Agrypnia crassicornis*: B, head; C, right anal proleg, dorsal view.   **D**: prothorax, ventral view, of *A. obsoleta*.

5　Prosternite present (arrow, Fig. 89D); (it may be hidden in the intersegmental fold and it is often very pale at instar II). Ventral surface of coxa of 2nd leg with some combs attached longitudinally (*lc*, Figs 91C, E)—　　　　　　　　　　Genus AGRYPNIA (part), 6

—　Prosternite absent. Ventral surface of coxa of 2nd leg with all combs attached transversely (as in Figs 92A, B)—

　　　　　　　　　　　　　　　　　　Genus PHRYGANEA, 8

　　Phryganea species are not separable at instar II: head width less than 0·75 mm, mesodorsum and metadorsum with only 1 seta at each anterior-lateral position.

6　Anterior margin of pronotum with a continuous transverse black band (Fig. 90B)—　　　　　　　(*Agrypnia obsoleta* and *A. varia*), 7

　　　These species are not separable at instar II: head width less than 0·65 mm, mesodorsum and metadorsum with only 1 seta at each anterior-lateral position).

—　Anterior margin of pronotum with two discrete patches of pigment (Fig. 90D)—　　　　　　　　**Agrypnia pagetana** Curtis

　　　　　　　　　　　　　　　　Agrypnia picta Kolenati

　　　These species may be separated on two characters. The fronto-clypeal band *fb* in *A. pagetana* is either of uniform width or widens slightly posteriorly (Fig. 90C) while in *A. picta* it is keyhole-shaped, widening markedly both anteriorly and posteriorly from a central constriction (Fig. 90E); Solem (1971) suggests that this difference will apply at instars II–V. The prosternite is dark in *A. pagetana* whilst in *A. picta* it is pale but has a bow-shaped posterior band which is usually very dark. (Characters for *A. picta* come from foreign material.)

　　　A. pagetana is a lowland species found in ponds, lakes and canals with emergent vegetation. It is widely distributed but is not recorded from northern Scotland. There are only two records of *A. picta*, both from the last century, and no specimens exist to confirm either record.

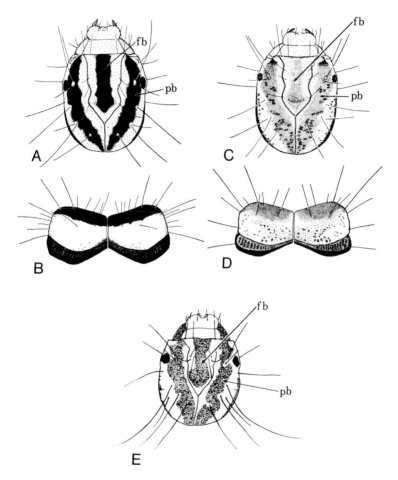

Fig. 90. **A, B**: *Phryganea bipunctata*: A, head; B, pronotum. **C, D**: *Agrypnia pagetana*: C, head; D, pronotum. **E**: head of *A. picta*.

7 Coxal combs of 1st and 2nd legs cover a broad area of the ventral
   surface (Figs 91B, C); on 2nd leg, combs are attached longitudinally
   or at an angle intermediate between longitudinal and transverse (Fig.
   91C); (rarely, a few extreme distal combs are transversely attached)—
   Agrypnia obsoleta (Hagen)
   Instars III to V

   At instar V, sometimes earlier, 7th abdominal segment has at least
   one dorsal gill and 8th abdominal segment normally has an anterior-
   lateral gill.

   A variety of permanent, still waters. Common; mainly upland areas in
   Scotland, northern England and Wales, more widespread in Ireland.

— Coxal combs of 1st and 2nd legs form a narrow band on the ventral
   surface (Figs 91D, E); on 2nd leg, combs are attached transversely,
   longitudinally, and at intermediate angles (Fig. 91E)—
   Agrypnia varia (Fabricius)
   Instars III to V

   7th abdominal segment with no dorsal gills; no gills on 8th abdominal
   segment.

   A variety of permanent, still waters. Widespread and common. Often
   replaced by *A. obsoleta* in upland waters.

Fig. 91. **A**: 1st leg, posterior view, of *Agrypnia obsoleta*. **B–E**: right coxa,
ventral view, showing arrangement of coxal combs: B, *A. obsoleta*, 1st
leg; C, *A. obsoleta*, 2nd leg; D, *A. varia*, 1st leg; E, *A. varia*, 2nd leg.

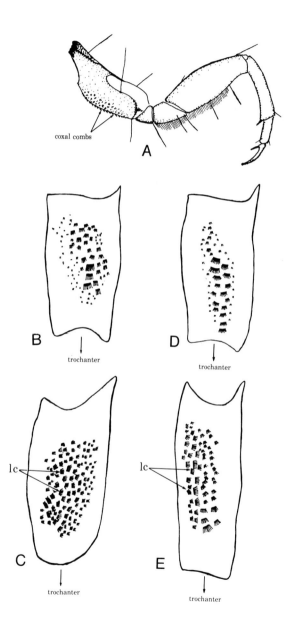

coxal combs

A

B

trochanter

D

trochanter

lc

C

trochanter

lc

E

trochanter

8(5) Well-developed coxal combs of 1st and 2nd legs arranged in 2–4 more or less regular longitudinal rows (Fig. 92A)—

Phryganea bipunctata Retzius
Instars III to V

At instars IV and V, mid-anterior pale patch of labrum does not extend back to the level of the two face setae and has a length:width ratio of about 1:4 (Fig. 92C).

Ponds, lakes and canals. Widespread and common.

— Well-developed coxal combs of 1st and 2nd legs arranged in 4 or more irregular longitudinal rows (Fig. 92B)—

Phryganea grandis L.
Instars III to V

At instars IV and V, mid-anterior pale patch of labrum extends back to the level of the two face setae and has a length:width ratio of about 1:2 (Fig. 92D).

Ponds, lakes and canals in lowland areas. Widespread.

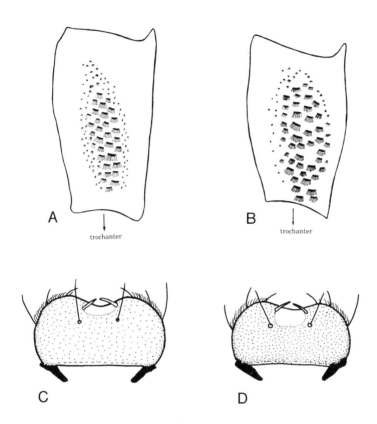

Fig. 92. **A, B**: coxa of 1st right leg, ventral view, showing arrangement of coxal combs: A, *Phryganea bipunctata*; B, *P. grandis*. **C**: labrum of *P. bipunctata*. **D**: labrum of *P. grandis*.

Family SERICOSTOMATIDAE

There are two British sericostomatids. The case of both species is curved and composed of sand grains (Fig. 93A), and is closed at the posterior end by a slightly conical membrane with a central hole (Fig. 93B).

The dorsal surface of the head has a flattened appearance and is dark brown in large larvae; very early instars have pale heads. The metadorsum has pale or colourless sclerites which, together with their associated setae, form two parallel transverse bands (Fig. 15G). This resembles the arrangement in *Odontocerum albicorne*, a species often found with *Sericostoma personatum*. Moreover, the anterior-lateral corner of the pronotum is sharply pointed in both species at later instars. Sericostomatids can be readily separated from *O. albicorne* by the form of the anal proleg claw, which has accessory hooks and a sharply angled crook (Figs 14C, D), and, except at instar II, by the presence of more than five setae on the anal proleg (excluding those on the claw, Figs 14A, B). In addition, the protrochantin is large with a hook-shaped tip (Figs 15B, C).

Small sericostomatid larvae superficially resemble the beraeid species *Beraea maurus, B. pullata,* and *Ernodes articularis* in the form of the case and the shape and colour of the head. However, the anal proleg has no ventral brush of setae (compare Figs 12F and 12H) or dorsal process and there is neither a sharp ridge nor a flap-like extension on the pronotum.

In Sericostomatidae, the number of larval instars appears to be variable. Elliott (1969) found six larval instars in *S. personatum* but Nielsen (1942) reported seven for the same species (as *S. pedemontanum* McLachlan). Resh *et al.* (1981) were able to induce up to fourteen instars in the North American sericostomatid *Gumaga nigricula* (McLachlan). The head widths of full-grown British sericostomatid larvae are about 1·5 mm in *N. ciliaris* and 2·00 mm in *S. personatum.*

Notidobia ciliaris flies in May and final instar larvae are found over winter. *Sericostoma personatum* has a more complicated life cycle (which has been studied by Elliott 1969) and final instar larvae may be present during much of the year.

Key to larvae

1   Head width more than 0·25 mm—   **2**

—   Head width less than 0·25 mm—   **Notidobia ciliaris** (L.)
                                             Sericostoma personatum (Spence)
                                                          Instar II (?)

2   Anterior-lateral corner of pronotum either prolonged (Fig. 93C) or
     angular (Figs 93D, E), never smoothly rounded. Ridge (arrow, Fig.
     93G) on lateral margin of dorsal surface of head is restricted to anterior
     region close to eye—   **Sericostoma personatum** (Spence)
                                             Instar III (?) to final instar

          Stony substratum in streams, rivers and lakes; also occasionally in
          spring streams and trickles. Widespread and common.

—   Anterior-lateral corner of pronotum smoothly rounded at all instars
     (Fig. 93F). Ridge (arrow, Fig. 93H) on lateral margin of dorsal
     surface of head continues posteriorly to coronal suture—
                                                Notidobia ciliaris (L.)
                                             Instar III (?) to final instar

          Associated with submerged roots of marginal vegetation in slow-
          flowing water. England north to Shropshire/Clwyd border and
          Nottinghamshire; local.

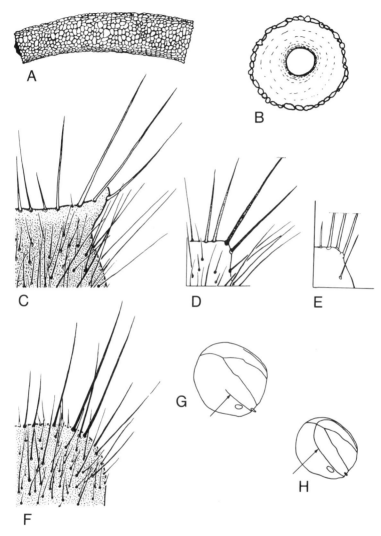

Fig. 93. **A, B**: case of *Sericostoma personatum*: A, lateral view; B, posterior end. **C–E**: right anterior-lateral corner of pronotum of *S. personatum*: C, final instar; D, early instar larva of head width o·55 mm; E, early instar larva of head width o·30 mm. **F**: right anterior-lateral corner of pronotum of *Notidobia ciliaris*. **G, H**: head capsule, dorso-lateral view: G, *S. personatum*; H, *N. ciliaris*.

ACKNOWLEDGEMENTS

We would like to thank those who have provided specimens or commented upon earlier versions of the keys, in particular Dr P. C. Barnard, Dr L. Botosaneanu, Dr M. I. Crichton, Mr D. A. Cooling, Miss S. Eldin, Mr G. Fretwell, Dr G. M. Gislason, Dr D. Harding, Dr A. G. Hildrew, Dr P. D. Hiley, Mr R. A. Jenkins, Dr J. P. O'Connor, Mrs M. Spirit, Professor G. B. Wiggins and Dr N. E. Williams.

Distribution records were extracted from the Scottish Insect Published Records Index at the National Museum of Scotland and the collections of the following Museums: British Museum (Natural History), Coventry, Liverpool, Manchester, National Museum of Scotland, Sheffield.

Professor R. B. Clark provided facilities for GNP at the University of Newcastle upon Tyne.

We are grateful to the authors and publishers of the following publications for permission to reproduce some of their drawings as the figures listed: Barnard (1971) 32D, E; Bray (1967) 89B, C, 90A–D, 91A, 92C, D (both modified); Edington & Hildrew (1981) 6A, C, 9A, B (all modified); Gislason (1979) 90E; Guidicelli & Vaillant (1967) 32F, J–L (all modified); Hickin (1967) 10D, 11F, 16A, C, 17A, 19C (modified), 20D, 33A, D, 35H, 47E, 51C, 69F, G, 70C, 71G, 74D, 84E, 85F–H, 87A (modified), 87D, 88B–D; Hiley (1972) 19A, 26A, 27A, B, 27C, D (both modified), 27F, 33B, C (both modified), 33E, F; Leader (1968) 86A–D; Lepneva (1970) 30A, B; Lepneva (1971) 7C, 10C, 71J, 72D, 75B, 84C, D, 87C, E, 89A; Mackereth (1956) 20C, 21C, D, 22C, 22D (modified), 23A; Murphy (1919) 19E, F; Nielsen (1942) 14I, 20A, B, E, F, 93A; Nielsen (1948) 28B, F, G, 29C, E, 31C, 32A (modified), 32C, G–I (all modified); Siltala (1907) 5A–C, 6D (modified), 28A (modified); Solem (1971) 7H, 89D, 91B–E, 92A, B; Wallace & Wallace (1985) 60C–E, 61D–L; Wallace (1977) 93C–F; Wallace et al. (1985) 81C–F, H; Wallace & Wiggins (1977) 88E–H; Wesenburg-Lund (1943) 26B; Wiberg-Larsen (1979) 10E, 12G, 16B, D–H, 17D–F, 18A–G; Wiggins (1977) 28D, 29D, 30C–E, 31A, B, D, E, 32B. Many other figures come from Hiley (1976) and Wallace (1980, 1981) and we are indebted to the Royal Entomological Society and the publishers of Freshwater Biology for permission to use them here. The figures drawn by Lepneva (listed above) are reproduced by kind permission of Keter Publishing House Jerusalem Ltd, Israel.

The plates of text-figures were prepared by Valerie Anderson of the Design Department, Liverpool Museum. Dr D. W. Sutcliffe edited and prepared the key for publication.

REFERENCES

Anderson, N. H. & Bourne, J. R. (**1974**). Bionomics of three species of glossosomatid caddis flies (Trichoptera : Glossosomatidae) in Oregon. *Can. J. Zool.* **52**, 405-411.

Barnard, P. C. (**1971**). The larva of *Agraylea sexmaculata* Curtis (Trichoptera, Hydroptilidae). *Entomologist's Gaz.* **22**, 253-257.

Barnard, P. C. (**1985**). An annotated check-list of the Trichoptera of Britain and Ireland. *Entomologist's Gaz.* **36**, 31-45.

Barnard, P. C. & O'Connor, J. P. (**1987**). The populations of *Apatania muliebris* McLachlan in the British Isles (Trichoptera : Limnephilidae). *Entomologist's Gaz.* **38**, 263-268.

Botosaneanu, L. (**1974**). Notes descriptives, faunistiques, écologiques, sur quelques trichoptères du "trio subtroglophile" (Insecta : Trichoptera). *Trav. Inst. Spéol. "Emile Racovitza"*, **13**, 61-75.

Bray, R. P. (**1964**). *Studies on the British Phryganeidae (Trichoptera) with special reference to the taxonomy and biology of the larvae.* Unpublished Ph.D. Thesis, University of Newcastle upon Tyne.

Bray, R. P. (**1966**). Records of the Phryganeidae (Trichoptera) in northern England 1961-1964, with a summary of the distribution of British species. *Trans. nat. Hist. Soc. Northumb.* **15**, 226-239.

Bray, R. P. (**1967**). The taxonomy of the larvae and pupae of the British Phryganeidae (Trichoptera). *J. Zool. Lond.* **153**, 223-244.

Denis, C. (**1984**). Fine structure of case-making larvae (Trichoptera). In *Proc. of the 4th int. Symp. Trichoptera, 1983*, 105-114. The Hague. Junk.

Disney, R. H. L. (**1972**). Larval Hydroptilidae (Trichoptera) that prey upon Simuliidae (Diptera) in Cameroon. *Entomologist's mon. Mag.* **108**, 84.

Edington, J. M. & Hildrew, A. G. (**1981**). A key to the caseless caddis larvae of the British Isles with notes on their ecology. *Scient. Publs Freshwat. Biol. Ass.* **43**, 1-92.

Elliott, J. M. (**1969**). Life history and biology of *Sericostoma personatum* (Spence) (Trichoptera). *Oikos* **20**, 110-118.

Elliott, J. M. (**1970**). The activity patterns of caddis larvae (Trichoptera). *J. Zool. Lond.* **160**, 279-290.

Elliott, J. M. (**1982**). A quantitative study of the life cycle of the case-building caddis *Odontocerum albicorne* (Trichoptera : Odontoceridae) in a Lake District stream. *Freshwat. Biol.* **12**, 241-255.

Fahy, E. (**1971**). The larva of *Hydroptila forcipata* (Eaton) (Trichoptera, Hydroptilidae). *Entomologist's mon. Mag.* **107**, 145-148.

Garside, A. (**1979**). A character separating the larvae of *Halesus radiatus* (Curtis) and *H. digitatus* (Schrank) (Trichoptera : Limnephilidae). *Entomologist's Gaz.* **30**, 137-139.

Gislason, G. M. (1979). Identification of Icelandic caddis larvae, with descriptions of *Limnephilus fenestratus* (Zett.) and *L. picturatus* McL. (Trichoptera : Limnephilidae, Phryganeidae). *Ent. scand.* **10**, 161-176.

Giudicelli, J. & Vaillant, F. (1967). La larve et la nymphe d'*Allotrichia pallicornis* (Eaton) (Trichoptera). *Trav. Lab. Hydrobiol. Piscic. Univ. Grenoble* **57-58**, 29-36.

Hanna, H. M. (1961). The larva of *Hydroptila sparsa* Curtis (Trichoptera : Hydroptilidae). *Entomologist's Gaz.* **12**, 69-75.

Hickin, N. E. (1967). *Caddis larvae. Larvae of the British Trichoptera.* London. Hutchinson. xi + 476 pp.

Hiley, P. D. (1972). The taxonomy of the larvae of the British Sericostomatidae (Trichoptera). *Entomologist's Gaz.* **23**, 105-119.

Hiley, P. D. (1976). The identification of British limnephilid larvae (Trichoptera). *Syst. Ent.* **1**, 147-167.

Jacquemart, S. (1962). La larve d'*Orthotrichia angustella* McL. (Trichoptère. Hydroptilidae). *Bull. Inst. r. Sci. nat. Belg.* **38**, 1-8.

Jacquemart, S. & Coineau, Y. (1962). Missions S. Jacquemart dans les Pyrénées orientals (2e note). Les Trichoptères Hydroptilides des Albères. *Bull. Inst. r. Sci. nat. Belg.* **38**, 1-181.

Jenkins, R. A. (1974). Occurrence of *Lasiocephala basalis* (Kolenati) (Trichoptera : Sericostomatidae) in a river in south-west Wales. *Entomologist's mon. Mag.* **110**, 83.

Kachalova, O. L. (1972). *Caddisflies (Trichoptera) of the rivers of Latvia.* Riga. 215 pp.

Kimmins, D. E. (1963). The British species of the genus *Mesophylax*, with further records of the occurrence of *Mesophylax aspersus* (Rambur) in Britain (Trichoptera, Limnephilidae). *Entomologist's Gaz.* **14**, 24-28.

Kimmins, D. E. (1966). A revised checklist of the British Trichoptera. *Entomologist's Gaz.* **17**, 111-120.

Leader, J. P. (1968). The larva of *Molanna palpata* MacLachlan, and some further characters of the larva of *Molanna angustata* Curtis (Trichoptera, Molannidae). *Entomologist's Gaz.* **19**, 21-29.

Lepneva, S. G. (1970). *Fauna of the U.S.S.R. Trichoptera 1, Larvae and Pupae of Annulipalpia.* Translation from 1964 Russian edition. Jerusalem. Israel Program for Scientific Translations. iv + 638 pp.

Lepneva, S. G. (1971). *Fauna of the U.S.S.R. Trichoptera 2, Larvae and Pupae of Integripalpia.* Translation from 1966 Russian edition. Jerusalem. Israel Program for Scientific Translations. iii + 700 pp.

Macan, T. T. (1973). A key to the adults of the British Trichoptera. *Scient. Publs Freshwat. Biol. Ass.* **28**, 1-151.

MacDonald, W. W. (1950). The larvae of *Mystacides azurea* L., *Cyrnus flavidus* McL. and *Oxyethira simplex* Ris (Trichoptera). *Proc. R. ent. Soc. Lond. (A)* **25**, 19-28.

Mackereth, J. C. (1956). Taxonomy of the larvae of the British species of the subfamily Glossosomatidae (Trichoptera). *Proc. R. ent. Soc. Lond. (A)* **31**, 167-172.

Marshall, J. E. (1978). Trichoptera : Hydroptilidae. *Handbk Ident. Br. Insects* I, **14** (a), 1-31.

Murphy, H. E. (1919). Observations on the egg-laying of the caddice-fly *Brachycentrus nigrisoma* Banks, and on the habits of the young larvae. *J. N. Y. ent. Soc.* **27**, 154-159.

Nielsen, A. (1942). Uber die Entwicklung und Biologie der Trichopteren mit besonderer Berucksichtigung der Quelltrichopteren Himmerlands. *Arch. Hydrobiol. (Suppl.)* **17**, 255-631.

Nielsen, A. (1948). Postembryonic development and biology of the Hydroptilidae. *Biol. Skr.* **5**, 1-200.

O'Connor, J. P. (1978). A progress report on studies of Irish Trichoptera. In: *Proc. of the 2nd Int. Symp. Trichoptera, 1977*, 303-308. The Hague. Junk.

O'Connor, J. P. (1980). *Limnephilus pati* sp. n. (Trichoptera : Limnephilidae), a caddisfly new to Great Britain and Ireland. *Ir. Nat. J.*, **20**, 129-133.

O'Connor, J. P. (1987). A review of the Irish Trichoptera. In: *Proc. of the 5th Int. Symp. Trichoptera, 1986*, 73-77. Dordrecht. Junk.

O'Connor, J. P. & Barnard, P. C. (1981). *Limnephilus tauricus* Schmid (Trichoptera : Limnephilidae) new to Great Britain, with a key to the *L. hirsutus* (Pictet) group in the British Isles. *Entomologist's Gaz.* **32**, 115-119.

O'Connor, J. P. & O'Hanrahan, B. M. (1988). *Agraylea sexmaculata* new to Ireland with notes on *Tricholeiochiton fagesii* and *Phacopteryx brevipennis* (Trichoptera). *Ir. Nat. J.*, **22**, 478-480.

Resh, V. H., Flynn, T. S., Lamberti, G. A., McElravy, E. P., Sorg, K. L. & Wood, J. R. (1981). Responses of the sericostomatid caddisfly *Gumaga nigricula* (McL.) to environmental disruption. In: *Proc. of the 3rd Int. Symp. Trichoptera, 1980*, 311-318. The Hague. Junk.

Ross, H. H. (1944). The caddisflies, or Trichoptera, of Illinois. *Bull. Ill. St. nat. Hist. Surv.* **23**, 1-326.

Siltala, A. J. (1907). Trichopterologische Untersuchungen. No. 2 Uber die postembryonale Entwicklung der Trichopteren-Larven. *Zool. Jahrb. Suppl.* **9** (2), 309-626, 1 pl.

Snodgrass, R. E. (1935). *Principles of insect morphology*. New York. McGraw-Hill. ix + 667 pp.

Solem, J. O. (1971). Larvae of the Norwegian species of *Phryganea* and *Agrypnia* (Trichoptera, Phryganeidae). *Norsk. ent. Tidsskr.* **18**, 79-88.

Solem, J. O. (1972). The larva of *Agraylea cognatella* McLachlan (Trichoptera, Hydroptilidae). *Norsk. ent. Tidsskr.* **19**, 77-79.

Wallace, B. & Wallace, I. D. (1985). A key to larvae of the genera *Micropterna* and *Stenophylax* (Trichoptera : Limnephilidae) in Britain and Ireland. *Entomologist's Gaz.* **36**, 127-133.

Wallace, I. D. (1976). *The taxonomy of larvae of the British species of the family Leptoceridae (Trichoptera), with notes on their general biology.* Unpublished Ph.D. Thesis, University of Newcastle upon Tyne.

Wallace, I. D. (1977). A key to larvae and pupae of *Sericostoma personatum* (Spence) and *Notidobia ciliaris* (Linné) (Sericostomatidae : Trichoptera) in Britain. *Freshwat. Biol.* **7**, 93-98.

Wallace, I. D. (1978). On distinguishing the larva of *Limnephilus elegans* Curtis in Britain (Trichoptera : Limnephilidae). *Entomologist's Gaz.* **29**, 177-178.

Wallace, I. D. (1980). The identification of British limnephilid larvae (Trichoptera : Limnephilidae) which have single-filament gills. *Freshwat. Biol.* **10**, 171-189.

Wallace, I. D. (1981). A key to larvae of the family Leptoceridae (Trichoptera) in Great Britain and Ireland. *Freshwat. Biol.* **11**, 273-297.

Wallace, I. D., Wallace, B. & O'Connor, J. P. (1985). The larva of *Limnephilus fuscinervis* (Trichoptera : Limnephilidae) with notes on the species' distribution and habitat in Ireland. *Ir. Nat. J.* **21**, 397-400.

Wallace, I. D. & Wiggins, G. B. (1978). Observations on the larva and pupa of the caddisfly genus *Hagenella* (Trichoptera : Phryganeidae). In: *Proc. of the 2nd Int. Symp. Trichoptera, 1977,* 165-173. The Hague. Junk.

Wesenberg-Lund, C. (1943). *Biologie der Susswasserinsekten.* J. Springer, Berlin. 682 pp.

Wiberg-Larsen, P. (1979). Revised key to larvae of Beraeidae in NW Europe (Trichoptera). *Ent. Scand.* **10**, 112-118.

Wiggins, G. B. (1977). *Larvae of the North American caddis fly genera (Trichoptera).* Toronto. University of Toronto Press. 401 pp.

INDEX

Page numbers in **bold** type indicate main key references. Redundant names are shown in parentheses.

PUBLICATIONS OF THE
FRESHWATER BIOLOGICAL ASSOCIATION

These publications and an up to date price list may be obtained direct from **Dept. DWS, Freshwater Biological Association, The Ferry House, Far Sawrey, Ambleside, Cumbria, LA22 0LP.**

SCIENTIFIC PUBLICATIONS

5. A KEY TO THE BRITISH SPECIES OF FRESHWATER CLADOCERA, by the late D. J. Scourfield & J. P. Harding, 3rd ed., 1966.   ISBN 0 900386 01 0

13. A KEY TO THE BRITISH FRESH- AND BRACKISH-WATER GASTROPODS, by T. T. Macan, 4th ed., 1977.   ISBN 0 900386 30 4

17. A KEY TO THE ADULTS AND NYMPHS OF THE BRITISH STONEFLIES (PLECOPTERA), by H. B. N. Hynes, 3rd ed., 1977. (Reprinted 1984).   ISBN 0 900386 28 2

18. A KEY TO THE BRITISH FRESHWATER CYCLOPID AND CALANOID COPEPODS, by J. P. Harding & W. A. Smith, 2nd ed., 1974.   ISBN 0 900386 20 7

20. A KEY TO THE NYMPHS OF BRITISH EPHEMEROPTERA, by T. T. Macan, 3rd ed., 1979.   ISBN 0 900386 35 5

23. A KEY TO THE BRITISH SPECIES OF FRESHWATER TRICLADS, by T. B. Reynoldson, 2nd ed., 1978.   ISBN 0 900386 34 7

25. SOME METHODS FOR THE STATISTICAL ANALYSIS OF SAMPLES OF BENTHIC INVERTEBRATES, by J. M. Elliott, 2nd ed., 1977.   ISBN 0 900386 29 0

27. A KEY TO BRITISH FRESHWATER FISHES, by Peter S. Maitland, 1972.
       ISBN 0 900386 18 5

29. TURBULENCE IN LAKES AND RIVERS, by I. R. Smith, 1975. ISBN 0 900386 21 5

30. AN ILLUSTRATED GUIDE TO AQUATIC AND WATER-BORNE HYPHOMYCETES (FUNGI IMPERFECTI), by C. T. Ingold, 1975.   ISBN 0 900386 22 3

31. A KEY TO THE LARVAE, PUPAE AND ADULTS OF THE BRITISH DIXIDAE (DIPTERA), by R. H. L. Disney, 1975.   ISBN 0 900386 23 1

32. A KEY TO BRITISH FRESHWATER CRUSTACEA MALACOSTRACA, by T. Gledhill, D. W. Sutcliffe & W. D. Williams, 1976.   ISBN 0 900386 24 X

33. DEPTH CHARTS OF THE CUMBRIAN LAKES, by A. E. Ramsbottom, 1976.
       ISBN 0 900386 25 8

34. AN ILLUSTRATED KEY TO FRESHWATER AND SOIL AMOEBAE, by F. C. Page, 1976.
       ISBN 0 900386 26 6

35. A KEY TO THE LARVAE AND ADULTS OF BRITISH FRESHWATER MEGALOPTERA AND NEUROPTERA, by J. M. Elliott, 1977.   ISBN 0 900386 27 4

36. WATER ANALYSIS: SOME REVISED METHODS FOR LIMNOLOGISTS, by F. J. H. Mackereth, J. Heron & J. F. Talling, 1978
(Second Impression, 1989).   ISBN 0 900386 31 2

37. A KEY TO THE ADULT MALES OF THE BRITISH CHIRONOMIDAE (DIPTERA), by L. C. V. Pinder, 1978. ISBN 0 900386 32 0

38. A KEY TO THE FRESHWATER PLANKTONIC AND SEMI-PLANKTONIC ROTIFERA OF THE BRITISH ISLES, by Rosalind M. Pontin, 1978. ISBN 0 900386 33 9

39. A GUIDE TO METHODS FOR ESTIMATING MICROBIAL NUMBERS AND BIOMASS IN FRESH WATER, by J. Gwynfryn Jones, 1979. ISBN 0 900386 37 1

40. A KEY TO THE BRITISH FRESHWATER LEECHES, by J. M. Elliott & K. H. Mann, 1979. ISBN 0 900386 38 X

41. A KEY TO THE BRITISH AND EUROPEAN FRESHWATER BRYOZOANS, by S. P. Mundy, 1980. ISBN 0 900386 39 8

42. DESMIDS OF THE ENGLISH LAKE DISTRICT, by Edna M. Lind & Alan J. Brook, 1980. ISBN 0 900386 40 1

43. CASELESS CADDIS LARVAE OF THE BRITISH ISLES, by J. M. Edington & A. G. Hildrew, 1981. ISBN 0 900386 41 X

44. A GUIDE TO THE MORPHOLOGY OF THE DIATOM FRUSTULE WITH A KEY TO THE BRITISH FRESHWATER GENERA, by H. G. Barber & E. Y. Haworth, 1981. ISBN 0 900386 42 8

45. A KEY TO THE LARVAE OF THE BRITISH ORTHOCLADIINAE (CHIRONOMIDAE), by P. S. Cranston, 1982. ISBN 0 900386 43 6

46. THE PARASITIC COPEPODA AND BRANCHIURA OF BRITISH FRESHWATER FISHES: A HANDBOOK AND KEY, by Geoffrey Fryer, 1982. ISBN 0 900386 44 4

47. A KEY TO THE ADULTS OF THE BRITISH EPHEMEROPTERA, by J. M. Elliott & U. H. Humpesch, 1983. ISBN 0 900386 45 2

48. KEYS TO THE ADULTS, MALE HYPOPYGIA, FOURTH-INSTAR LARVAE AND PUPAE OF THE BRITISH MOSQUITOES (CULICIDAE), by P. S. Cranston, C. D. Ramsdale, K. R. Snow & G. B. White, 1987. ISBN 0 900386 46 0

49. LARVAE OF THE BRITISH EPHEMEROPTERA: A KEY WITH ECOLOGICAL NOTES, by J. M. Elliott, U. H. Humpesch & T. T. Macan, 1988. ISBN 0 900386 47 9

50. ADULTS OF THE BRITISH AQUATIC HEMIPTERA HETEROPTERA: A KEY WITH ECOLOGICAL NOTES, by A. A. Savage, 1989. ISBN 0 900386 48 7

OCCASIONAL PUBLICATIONS

1. A SYNONYMIC AND BIBLIOGRAPHIC CHECK-LIST OF THE FRESHWATER MITES (HYDRA-CHNELLAE AND LIMNOHALACARIDAE, ACARI) RECORDED FROM GREAT BRITAIN AND IRELAND, by T. Gledhill & K. O. Viets, 1976.

5. A BIBLIOGRAPHY OF WORKS FOR THE IDENTIFICATION OF FRESHWATER INVERTEBRATES IN THE BRITISH ISLES, by P. D. Armitage, M. T. Furse & J. F. Wright, 1979.

7. LIST OF PUBLICATIONS OF THE FRESHWATER BIOLOGICAL ASSOCIATION 1929-1978, by I. Pettman, 1979.

8. A SEASONAL RECORD OF THE NUTRIENT CHEMISTRY OF WINDERMERE FOR 1931-1932, by Penelope M. Jenkin & W. Davison, 1979.

9. A PRELIMINARY DESK STUDY OF PETROLEUM HYDROCARBONS IN FRESH WATERS, by J. G. Jones, J. E. M. Horne, Pamela Moorhouse & Deborah L. Powell, 1980.

10. ENVIRONMENTAL EFFECTS OF DEFORESTATION: AN ANNOTATED BIBLIOGRAPHY, by J. R. Blackie, E. D. Ford, J. E. M. Horne, D. J. J. Kinsman, F. T. Last & P. Moorhouse, 1980.

13. INVESTIGATIONS ON PHYTOPLANKTON WITH SPECIAL REFERENCE TO WATER USAGE, by J. W. G. Lund, 1981.

14. PROVISIONAL ATLAS OF THE FRESHWATER LEECHES OF THE BRITISH ISLES, by J. M. Elliott & P. A. Tullett, 1981.

15. THE JENKIN SURFACE-MUD SAMPLER: USER MANUAL, by F. R. Ohnstad & J. G. Jones, 1982.

16. CONCENTRATIONS OF MAJOR IONS IN LAKES AND TARNS OF THE ENGLISH LAKE DISTRICT (1953-1978), by T. R. Carrick & D. W. Sutcliffe, 1982.

17. ECOLOGY OF FREE-LIVING PROTOZOA: A BIBLIOGRAPHY, by B. J. Finlay & C. Ochsenbein-Gattlen, 1982.

18. AQUATIC MACROPHYTES IN THE TARNS AND LAKES OF CUMBRIA, by R. Stokoe, 1983.

19. RECORDS FROM THE AUTOMATIC FISH COUNTER ON THE RIVER FROME, DORSET, 1970-1981, by R. H. K. Mann, J. M. Hellawell, W. R. C. Beaumont & G. I. Williams, 1983.

20. A SUPPLEMENT TO A BIBLIOGRAPHY OF SAMPLERS FOR BENTHIC INVERTEBRATES, by J. M. Elliott & P. A. Tullett, 1983.

21. CONCENTRATIONS OF MAJOR IONS IN STREAMS ON CATCHMENTS OF THE RIVER DUDDON (1971-1974) AND WINDERMERE (1975-1978) ENGLISH LAKE DISTRICT, by T. R. Carrick & D. W. Sutcliffe, 1983.

22. THE FBA AIR-LIFT SAMPLER; USER MANUAL, by C. M. Drake, B. Winstanley, F. R. Ohnstad & J. M. Elliott, 1983.

23. ENVIRONMENTAL EFFECTS OF CADMIUM IN FRESH WATER: A BIBLIOGRAPHY, by J. Wallen, A. S. Wightman & W. Penning, 1984.

24. LAKE DISTRICT WATERS: AN INDEX AND BIBLIOGRAPHY OF SCIENTIFIC RESEARCH, by J. Wallen, A. S. Wightman & W. Penning, 1984.

25. BIBLIOGRAPHY ON THE HYDRAULIC RESISTANCE OR ROUGHNESS OF VEGETATED WATER COURSES, by F. H. Dawson & F. G. Charlton, 1988.

26. WATER TEMPERATURE DATA FROM STREAMS & RIVERS IN N. EASTERN ENGLAND, by D. T. Crisp, 1988.

27. THE FBA FREEZE SAMPLER: USER MANUAL, by P. A. Carling & J. Crompton, 1988.